S0-FPI-000

EVERYDAY LETTERING AND PRINTING

EVERYDAY LETTERING AND PRINTING

Terry Harvey

Evans

Evans Brothers Limited London

Published by Evans Brothers Limited,
Montague House, Russell Square,
London, W.C.1

© Terry Harvey 1973

First published 1973

All Rights Reserved. No part of this publication may be
reproduced, stored in a retrieval system, or transmitted,
in any form, or by any means, electronic, mechanical,
photocopying, recording or otherwise, without the
prior permission of Evans Brothers Limited.

Set in 11 on 13 point Imprint by
Keyspools Ltd, Golborne, Lancashire
and printed in Great Britain by
C Tinling & Co Ltd, Prescot and London

ISBN 0 237 44597 2   PRA 3388

CONTENTS

Introduction	6
Hand lettering	7
Stencils	29
Instant lettering	43
Printing	51
Layout	77
Appendix 1 Costs	92
Appendix 2 Suppliers	94

INTRODUCTION

This book is intended for anyone without a great deal of time, money and expertise who is called upon fairly regularly to turn out effective and eye-catching notices for display. Teachers, shopkeepers, youth leaders, administrators, clergymen, librarians, managers, union officials and the local Mothers' Union Secretary must advertise, cancel, inform, request and remind. Their output can range from the small notice stating the price of apples in the corner shop to the wholesale labelling of the School Open Day Exhibition. It may well be possible to have the work done professionally, but there comes a time when such a course of action is too expensive, too cumbersome or too late. People who produce notices and displays usually do so as a by-product of their main occupation and have not had the practice to achieve the standards of the commercial artist or printer, assuming that such standards are always appropriate. The label which will be used once for a limited period hardly warrants the same care as the permanent sign.

I have not attempted to argue the case for clear and attractive lettering, presuming that anyone picking up this book will have that motivation, anyway. All I have attempted to do is to bring together a number of methods, materials and approaches that I have found useful and which fulfil the three basic requirements hinted at above.

The first is speed, which generally overrides considerations of quality and finish, but need not do so. The second is low cost. A display typesetter produces quick and beautiful results, but the four-figure price is for most people not only prohibitive, but actually in the realms of fantasy. The third is simplicity of production. Each of the processes described has been used not only by adults but also by children in school and has proved successful both in the standard of results obtained and in the enjoyment obtained from the activity itself.

HAND LETTERING

The quickest and cheapest method is lettering by hand. The simplicity of the operation depends upon the amount of time one is prepared to put into practising the letter shapes, and developing the facility, since it is possible with practice to print a presentable alphabet almost as quickly as one can print normally. The commercial artist develops these skills as part of his technique and the results are often indistinguishable from the printed letter.

There is no sleight-of-hand or special talent required for the making of acceptable lettering. All that you need is a good model to work from and some determination and perseverance. Before explaining that remark, I think we should look quickly at some examples of printer's jargon I intend to use frequently, since it will establish a useful verbal shorthand.

All letters are either capitals or small letters, but since one can also have small capitals, I shall use the term 'caps' for capitals (these are sometimes referred to as 'upper case') and 'lower case' for small letters. As a combination, speaking of 'large lower case letters' is perhaps less confusing than 'large small letters'.

A lettering designer creates an alphabet using a recognisable series of shapes whose proportions differ very slightly from any other known design. The proportion of width of stroke to height of letter and the amount of air-space left in and around the letter are two of the elements which give the letters the distinctive character known as its 'face'. The type-founder labels each face with a name, in many cases perpetuating the name of the designer. Bodoni, Baskerville and Gill are three such names. Some faces have a distinctly 'printed' look, Figs. 1, 2 and 3, whilst others look as though they could be derived from pen or brush originals. Figs. 4, 5, 6 and 7.

Until comparatively recently in the history of type design, the original shapes on which designers have drawn have been made with either pen or chisel. The square

Fig. 1

ABCdef

Fig. 2

ABCD

Fig. 3

ABC

Fig. 4

ABCDEFG

Fig. 5

abcdefghi

Fig. 6

abcde

Fig. 7

abcdef

Fig. 8

ABC

pen makes a thick or thin mark depending upon the direction of stroke, and the chisel forces the sculptor to cut more than once per stroke in order to obtain the necessary visual weight. The Romans developed their letter forms to a highly sophisticated degree, and their sculptors added an extra flourish when finishing off the foot of a letter. This additional mark is the 'serif', and is found on almost all faces designed before this present century. Designers ignored or perhaps failed to realise the importance of the map-maker's etching tool or the invention of the metal pen nib with its uniform line in the nineteenth century, and lettering continued to exhibit the same characteristics—thick and thin lines and serifs. This is the classical face. Modern designers, however, have followed the lead of Eric Gill in the creation of lettering both uniform of stroke and without serifs. This type of letter is called 'san-serif'. We now have the situation where the type designer has a choice of thick or thin marks or a combination of both, and

Fig. 9

ABCDE

Fig. 10

ABCDEFG

he may, or may not, use serifs. Figs. 8, 9, and 10.

'Condensed' lettering is a self-explanatory term. It is useful on occasions to be able to cram a large number of letters into a short space or make a long word taller. Fig. 11a and b.

'Italic' is a name given not only to a style of handwriting but more precisely to lettering which leans from the vertical.

Most faces are available in all these variations—the straightforward letter, the condensed, a 'light' or thin version, a 'bold' or thick version and italic. This gives an enormous number of possibilities from which to choose a model. Figs. 12, 13 and 14.

12

Fig. 11a

abcdefghij

Fig. 11b

ABCDEFGH

Fig. 12

ABCDE

Fig. 13

abcde

Fig. 14

abcde

Fig. 15    Fig. 16

ABC ABC

14

Fig. 17

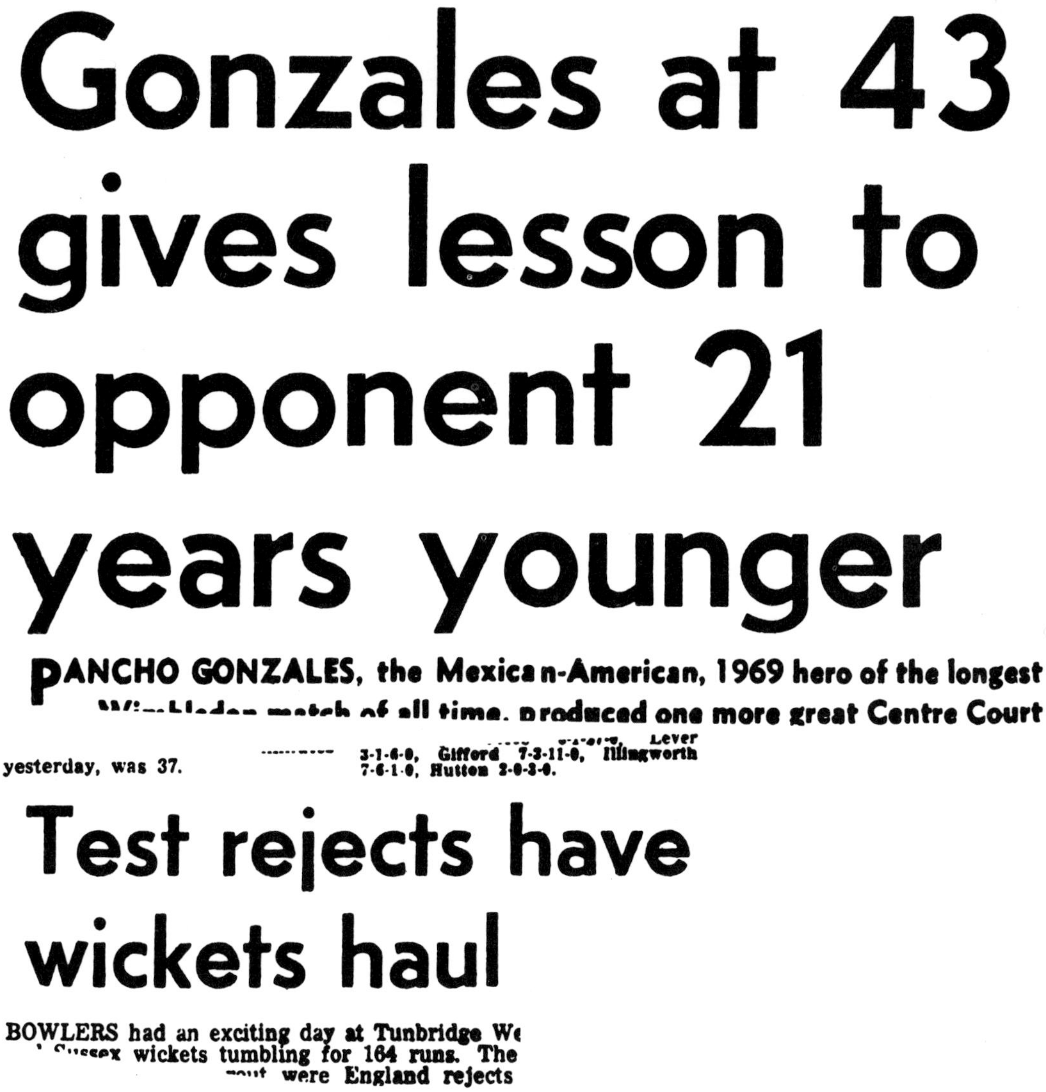

Gonzales at 43 gives lesson to opponent 21 years younger

PANCHO GONZALES, the Mexican-American, 1969 hero of the longest Wimbledon match of all time, produced one more great Centre Court yesterday, was 37.

3-1-6-0, Gifford 7-3-11-0, Illingworth 7-6-1-0, Hutton 2-0-3-0.
Lever

Test rejects have wickets haul

BOWLERS had an exciting day at Tunbridge We Sussex wickets tumbling for 164 runs. The were England rejects

Working from a model

Set out to find a face which looks as though it will translate back into hand-drawn characters. You can find in any magazine or newspaper a long heading or subheading in a size sufficiently large for the shapes to be clearly seen. These samples came from the same page of a newspaper, and there are enough letters to give you a large proportion of the alphabet. Fig. 17.

There are also books of alphabets available which are primarily demonstrating

Fig. 18

abcd
efghi
klmn

vpqr
styvj
oxuz

trends in design, but which provide very valuable models; there are type-founders' catalogues, and the 'instant lettering' firms provide catalogues of their products which are not only valuable in themselves but are also exactly suited to our present purpose. Fig. 18.

I would suggest that you use a square-ended felt-tipped marker to begin with. This, you will find, imposes its own conditions. Make a mark like a continuous

Fig. 19

'w' with it, and then try a continuous loop. Fig. 19.

Fig. 20

Hold the pen firmly with the square edge at the same angle to the paper all the time. You may even find it helpful to keep the wrist and hand rigid and move the whole of the forearm.

Assuming that you are right-handed, the mark will be thicker on the down stroke than the up, and will vary smoothly from thick to thin on the curve.

The lettering you are looking for as a model, then, could be a classical face, but try to find a 'thick-and-thin' face without serifs, or ignore the serifs on the face you find. It is not because serifs are difficult to draw; it is simply that they will initially distract you from the main purpose, which is understanding the *shape* of the letter you are studying, and they take up time, thus defeating the overall purpose of the exercise.

Copy the easier letters first—the m and n,

v and w; try the h and j and then try to analyse the letter c and its derivatives b, d, p and q, possibly even g and o. Watch the proportion of width of stroke to height of letter and the open or closed quality of the shape. Observe the position of the thin parts of the letter—does this indicate to you how to hold the felt pen? In the example given here, for instance, the pen would have to be held at right angles to the bottom of the page, instead of at forty-five degrees to it as is normal.

Try to find a way of holding the tool you are writing with in as comfortable a way as possible and in your normal writing position.

Finally, have a go at the more difficult, but much more rewarding, letters like a, e, f, r, t and k and finish off with s. This letter generally gives more trouble than all the rest because people do not believe their eyes. It really does start *there* and snake backwards and forwards and wind half-way up to the top again! Fig. 20. Copy the individual letters, repeating

Fig. 21

Fig. 22

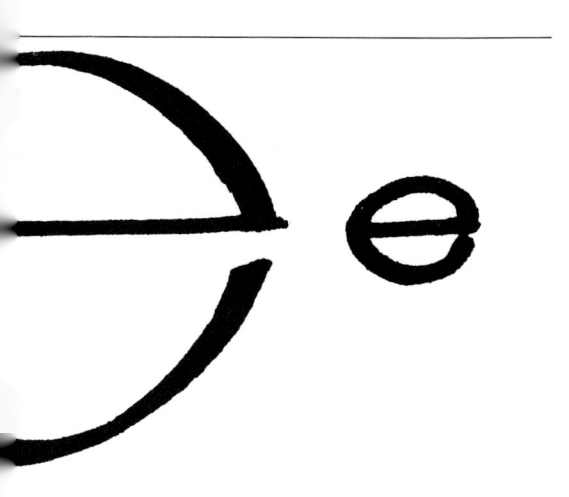

until you get as close to the original as possible then try repeating the more difficult or characteristic shapes until the desired consistency is reached and try varying the size. Fig. 21.

Put letters together to form convenient practice words. Your lettering will then have a consistency of style and size, and some of the character of the original face will be retained. Fig. 22.

Ignore complicated shapes, scripts and especially 'Old English'—they take up

Fig. 23

too much time unless you already have a range of other faces and a special occasion. Fig. 23.

Spend about fifteen minutes to half an hour a day practising this for a week. At the end of this time you should have been through the alphabet two or three times. During the next week try putting the letters together to form words, *but refer constantly to the master* to ensure that you are using the correct shapes. Try, during the second week, to memorise the shapes, and spend the third week memorising and checking the shapes again. By this time you ought to be quite proficient, but keep to the same face for some weeks until you feel the need to add to your repertoire. I find that for most purposes I rarely need more than one basic face and a decorative one. The important point is that you must often refer to your basic alphabet to *refine* the shapes that you have learned, since the chances are that you will not have understood the shape properly first time.

Fig. 24a

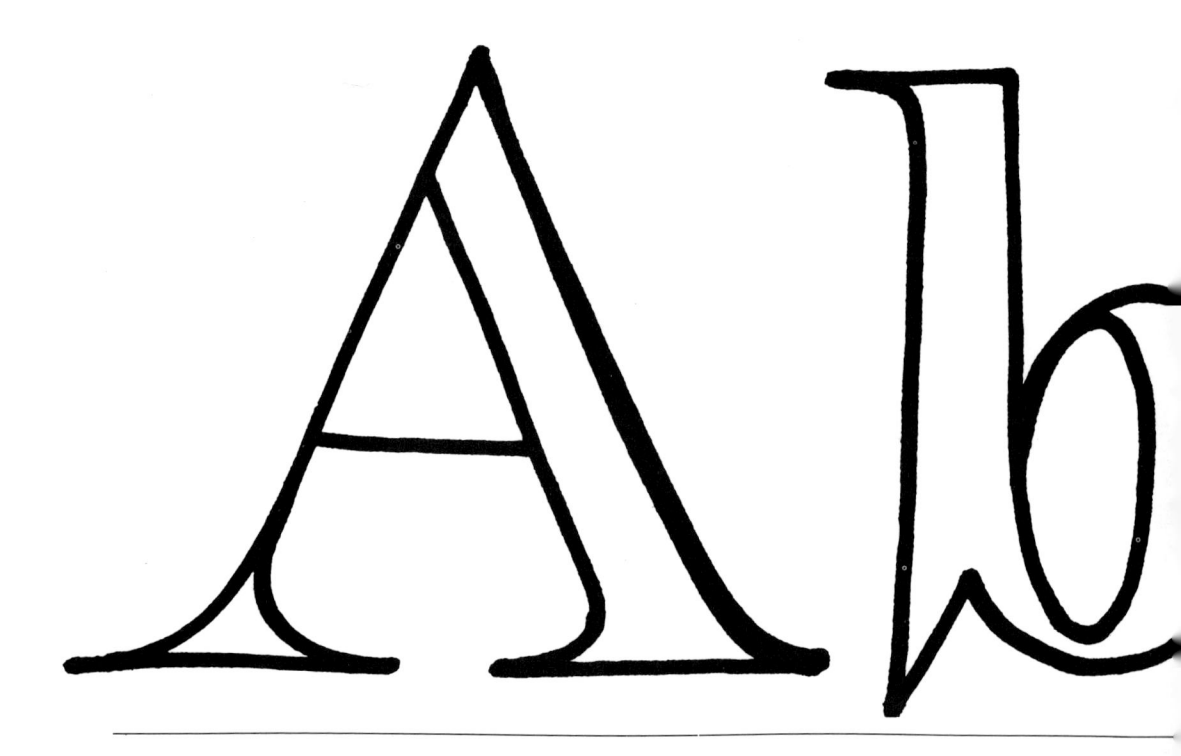

eam

When you are bored with this alphabet, use the variations—light and bold, condensed and italic. Combine these first to give your products uniformity of style.

Then consider trying out another alphabet. This one will be much easier to learn, since you are concentrating on the *difference* between this and your first model. Many letters will be quite similar. For a real change, however, you might consider an outline letter. This will help in your understanding of letter con-

Fig. 24b

struction and in the control of your hand, and will also prove to be one way of producing large letters with a minimum of effort. The outline letter has visually more weight than the simple line version, and is easier to read. Fig. 24a and b.

Outline letters are not only fun to do, but superlative exercises in construction, and reveal more than any other method the structure of the face. They are also useful for producing in very large sizes optically solid letters without the time or trouble needed to fill in an outline. They save paint, too!

Fig. 25

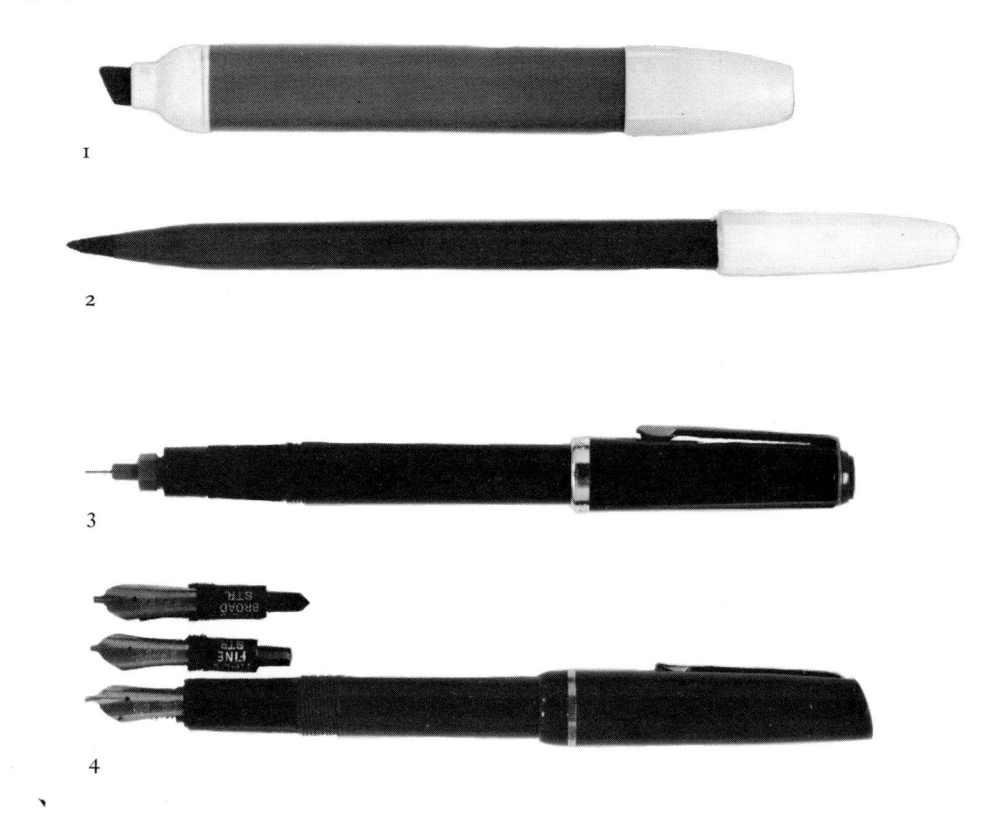

1

2

3

4

Tools

The tool used can affect the impact of the letters and can also help to convey a mood if this is important. You can get good and varied results from pencils and ball-point pens, markers and felt-tipped pens, square pens and ball-ended pens and by virtually anything which will make a mark.

Lettering pens with a felt nib and a wooden shank can be obtained from E. J. Arnold and Son Ltd. (see Appendix 2). These have the advantage that after use with paint they can be cleaned with water ready for next time. They can also be used with a variety of coloured inks, thus cutting down on the number of regular felt tipped pens you need to buy. The photograph, Fig. 25, shows two examples of the ready-filled felt pen, 1 and 2, which are universally available. The special lettering pen, 3, is for use either with stencils or in freehand lettering. This fills in the same way as a

27

Fig. 26

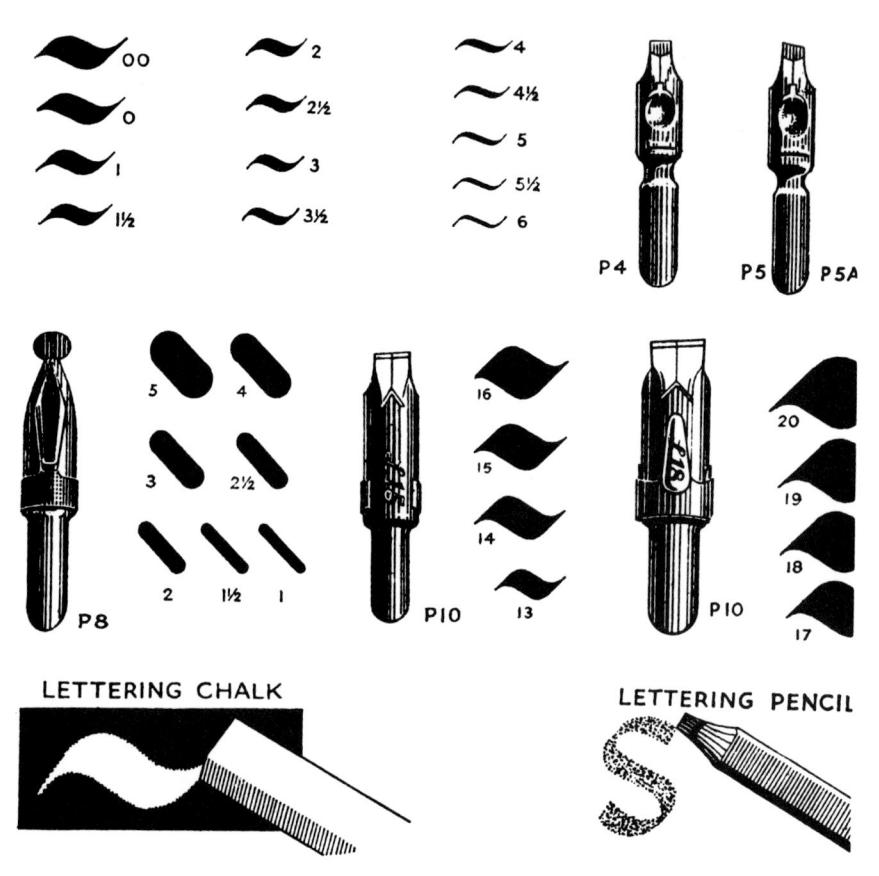

conventional fountain pen, 4, which has the advantage of having a range of interchangeable nibs both round and square-ended in a variety of widths.

The catalogues of firms supplying art materials to schools are always worth having a look at as they provide a fund of ideas and possibilities. Fig. 26.

Finally, it is worth stressing that a hand-written letter will never look as polished as a printed one, so one must arrive at a compromise. However, learning an alphabet in the way I have suggested will at least ensure that the hand-written letter will look uniform in design and execution, and some of the character of the original face will pervade the finished result.

STENCILS

abc123
ABC
abcd
1234

ABC
1234
ABC
abcde
1234

Fig. 1

FR

I am not suggesting that stencils are intrinsically better than hand-drawn letters. They perform a slightly different function. All lettering produced by or closely resembling printing processes is by definition more formal than hand lettering and is therefore less personal. It is used for more permanent notices, more formal purposes, or for those occasions where the individual stamp of the hand-drawn letter would be inappropriate.

The printed or duplicable letter also introduces two new elements; the possibility of fairly exact mass-production and, for teachers, the involving of the child in school. All the methods described in this chapter are suitable for use by children.

The governing factor in the choice of stencil is that of price, since all stencils are the same in principle, differing only in ruggedness of construction, precision or range. It is possible to buy wax impregnated paper stencils for a few pence or lay out several pounds for a wide range of plastic stencils in a box complete with paints and brushes.

The simplest stencil is the wax paper stencil and the easiest method of application is to use a stubby brush and hammer the paint on to the paper. They are generally available in one or two inch caps, and a very nice Victorian style is also on the market, which is rather overpowering in bulk, but attractive when used as contrast.

The sort of results you get from the average stencil are to be found on any self-respecting crate or tea chest. Visually, the limitation is imposed by the construction bars which break up the letters but which are necessary to hold the shapes together. Fig. 1.

Fig. 2

More sophisticated stencils attempt to overcome this problem in different ways. One way is to require the user to draw only an outline or to use a pen specially designed for that particular stencil. Here are some possibilities, taken from the catalogue of a stencil manufacturer, Uno. Fig. 2.

There is a remarkable range of lettering available in this sort of stencil. The number of faces is increasing rapidly and the usual variants of light, bold, condensed and italic are supplemented by some others peculiar to the stencil technique. Once again a browse through the catalogues will provide you with ideas.

32

Fig. 3

ABCDEFG
HIJKLMN
1234aübcd
efghijklm

A second way of overcoming the problem of construction bars is to design the stencil so that the bars are involved in the design. This is particularly successful and pleasing in a pen-derived style where the bar is inserted in the thinnest part of the letter. This example is from the Standardgraph range. Fig. 3.

Fig. 4

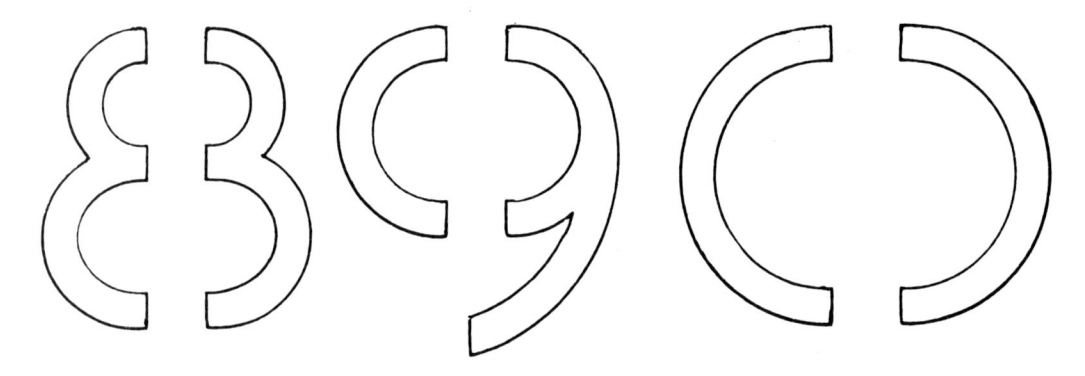

890

A third way of avoiding the bar is to split the divided letter distinctly into two pieces, so that the stencil has to be moved to complete the letter. An Econasign example is shown in Fig. 4.

Fig. 5

Fig. 6

A different type of stencil, and perhaps the most successful in its avoidance of bar problems, is a solid *individual* letter made from plastic or wood. In this case, the user draws round the outside and inside of the letter. Upper and lower case letters are available as well as figures. The lettering can be left as an outline, can be filled in or treated in several ways. Figs. 5 and 6.

This lettering is also useful in informal, if still impersonal, ways. The example in Fig. 5 has been drawn around, roughly filled say with a line from a coloured felt marker and the outline overdrawn with short straight lines (even round the curves). The impact is stronger than with the simpler methods.

35

PLASTIC letters

Perhaps the most colourful possibility is in the use of these letters with inks and a mouth spray Fig. 7a. The letters are arranged in the desired order and sprayed over with any kind of ink or thin paint, using an extremely cheap mouth spray. Aerosols produce a still better result, but they are comparatively expensive. Fig. 7b.

When spraying, make sure that the tubes of the spray are kept clean and free, are washed out after use, and that the tubes themselves are at right angles to each other. Best results are achieved with the spray at about 18–24 inches from the job, when the drops of ink are thoroughly atomised and at their finest. The closer one gets to the paper the bigger and cruder the drops of colour become, the spray becomes more difficult to control and one risks spoiling the work with large drops falling at random. Properly controlled, the results are eye-catching and in the classroom the process is a source of

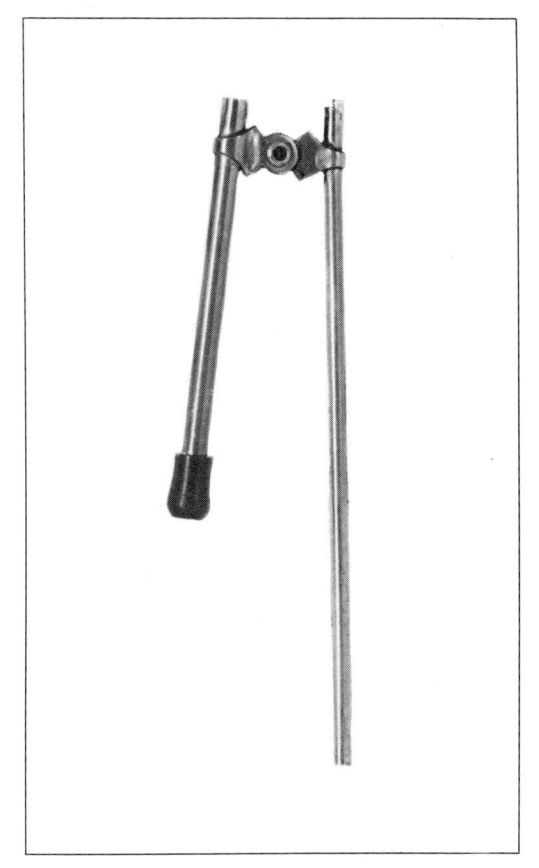

Fig. 7a   Fig. 7b

delight to children. A word of warning here, however. To obtain the force required to atomise the ink one blows hard enough to build up what feels like a fair amount of pressure in the head. An adult has sufficient awareness to know when to stop, but enthusiastic children tend to go past this point with calamitous and possibly serious results. I have had in class several children with mild headaches and one blackout. This method has to be closely watched. I might point out that these occurrences are sufficiently rare to be almost discounted, and are negligible when compared with the pleasure children get from it, and the quality of the results.

Traced letters
I have left the traced letter until now, because it is rather difficult to know how to categorise it, since it is partly a mechanical technique, capable of mass-production on a small scale, and partly a

Fig. 8

hand-drawn letter. It produces unusual and elegant results, but takes more care and time than the conventional stencil, as more steps are involved.

First of all, as with hand-drawn lettering, one must find a model, but this time the model is to be traced, so it must be exactly the right size needed for the final job. Using a standard tracing paper or a greaseproof wrapping paper, trace the letters, arranging them as required. These can be transferred to the final surface by rubbing the flat of a pencil over the drawn outlines of the individual letters on the *back* of the tracing paper and re-drawing the letters. To avoid confusion, I have found it useful to draw the first copy in, say, a blue ball-point and re-trace in red or black. Then one can always tell at a glance which parts have been re-traced. Instead of the pencil rubbing, one could use carbon paper, but this is rather less precise in operation and tends to leave unwanted marks on the paper. Fig. 8.

OMES
and gardens
issue - out now!

ELVES

It might also be worth mentioning here that should enormous lettering ever be required (sports day banners, marquee identification etc.), stencils can be enlarged using either the overhead projector or the epidiascope. In this way a two-inch stencil can be made to yield a two metre letter, very quickly and most accurately. This is probably the fastest way of obtaining large-scale lettering. An industrial variation in use for the lettering of large vehicles and pantechnicons is the projection of a 35mm slide transparency of the original art work. This is projected on to the side of the vehicle and traced around. The advantages are that if a distinctive style of letter is being used or the firm is repeating its house style (as on its letter headings and trade-marks), this can be painted on a variety of vehicle sizes simply by rearranging the projection distance.

Fig. 9

STUDIO
STUDIO

Finally, a guide to spacing may be of use. The only requirement of hand lettering is that it must conform to the standards expected of the printed word. The history of printing has been one of a continuous refinement of the design and mechanics of the individual letter to allow machine spacing to become as close to the aesthetically desirable as possible, and although the process is not yet perfect, the compromise situation we have today is of a very high standard. We are, these days, so unaccustomed to seeing badly spaced words and letters even in our speedily-produced newspapers and magazines that we immediately recognise the occasional example as being distinctly 'wrong'. It may well be possible to produce definitive mathematical relationships between uprights, horizontals and curves, but the simple rule of thumb is that the air-space between any two letters must be *optically* the same as between the other letters. This means in practical terms that it is not useful to measure the *distance* between letters, since two uprights one centimetre apart will look closer than two curves at the same distance. One must adjust all the letters until the gaps between *look* similar. Fig. 9.

It is possible to develop a healthy obsession about spacing, since it is only with experience that one develops the taste for good spacing. After a while, the eye begins to see many subtleties that are normally overlooked and one sees through the printer's compromises with his type.

However, both the printer and the professional layout artist are well ahead of the layman in recognising the limitations of the craft and, where time and expense permits, sentences and paragraphs as well as individual letters are adjusted to harmonise with each other rhythmically until the mundane job of printing becomes the art of typography.

INSTANT LETTERING

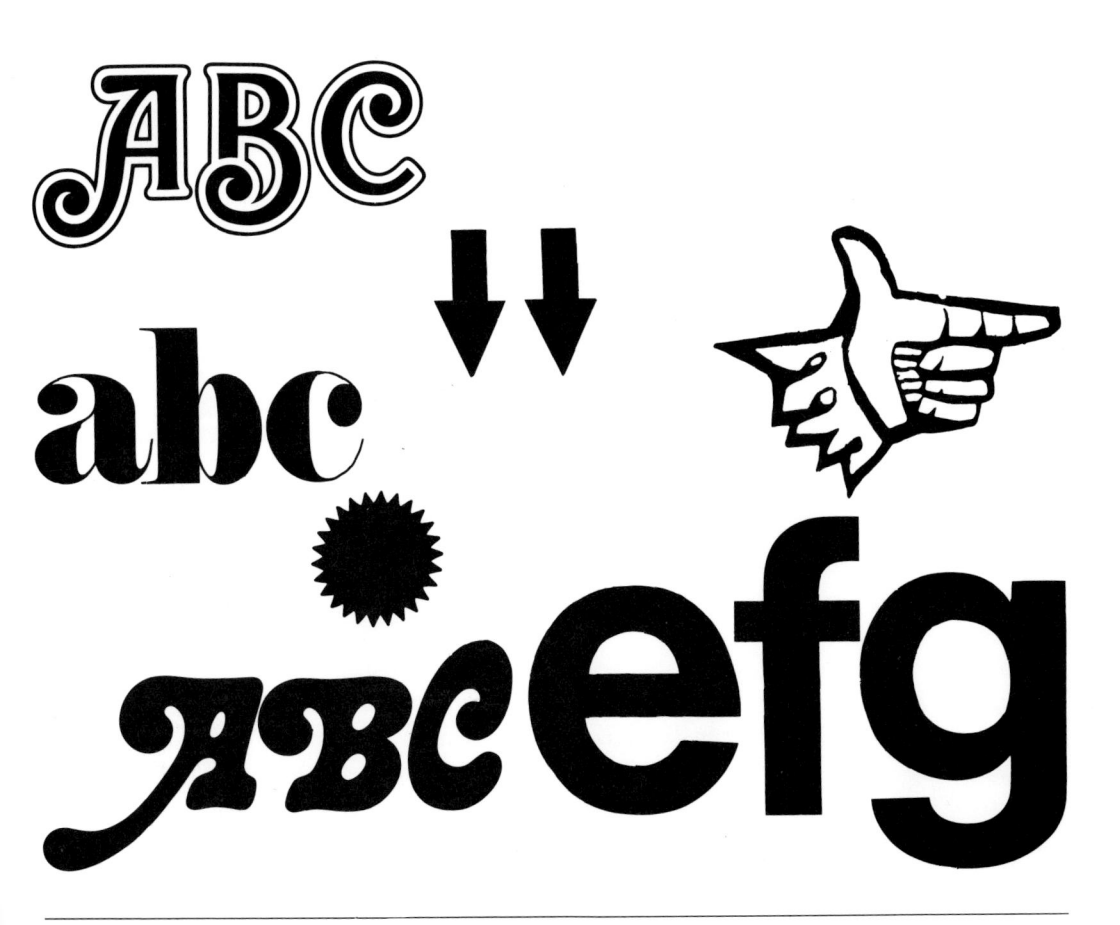

Fig. 1

Instant Lettering is very much a child of our time. *For the one-off job*, here is a quality and a variety undreamed of by Gutenberg or Caxton and at a price that the printer cannot touch.

Letters are printed on a specially treated plastic sheet and may be transferred to virtually any desired surface simply by rubbing over with a ball-point pen. The method involves no more than that—there is no soaking or wetting or removal of a support; the system is one of dry transfer. The letters may be attached to paper, board, wood, glass, skin, golf balls, plastics, metals and even some fabrics. The list is almost endless.

Instant lettering is quite simple to use. Obviously practice helps, but quite impressive results are possible at first attempt if care is taken. Begin by removing the protective backing. Lay this on one side and replace the lettered sheet on it whenever this sheet is put down. This helps to prevent any possibility of the

Fig. 2

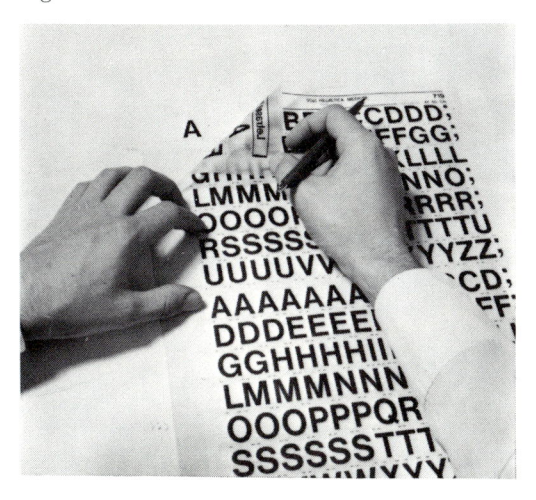

Fig. 3

lettering transferring accidentally, and although this may not affect the working surface, it is worth remembering that instant lettering once used, is not recoverable, so every transferred letter (or part of a letter) has cost you money. Since the sheet of lettering is transparent it can be easily manoeuvred into position. Rub the letter in question gently with the thumb to locate it and then rub lightly with a moderately pointed object (a worn-out ball pen works nicely, as does a pencil) until the letter changes from black to a uniform grey. Fig. 1. The sheet can then be removed carefully, revealing the first letter stuck down. Fig. 2. The second letter is then moved into place and the process continues. When each word is finished it is advisable to burnish the lettering slightly by placing the backing sheet over the word and rubbing gently with the *side* of a ball point, for instance. This helps to secure the lettering finally. Fig. 3.

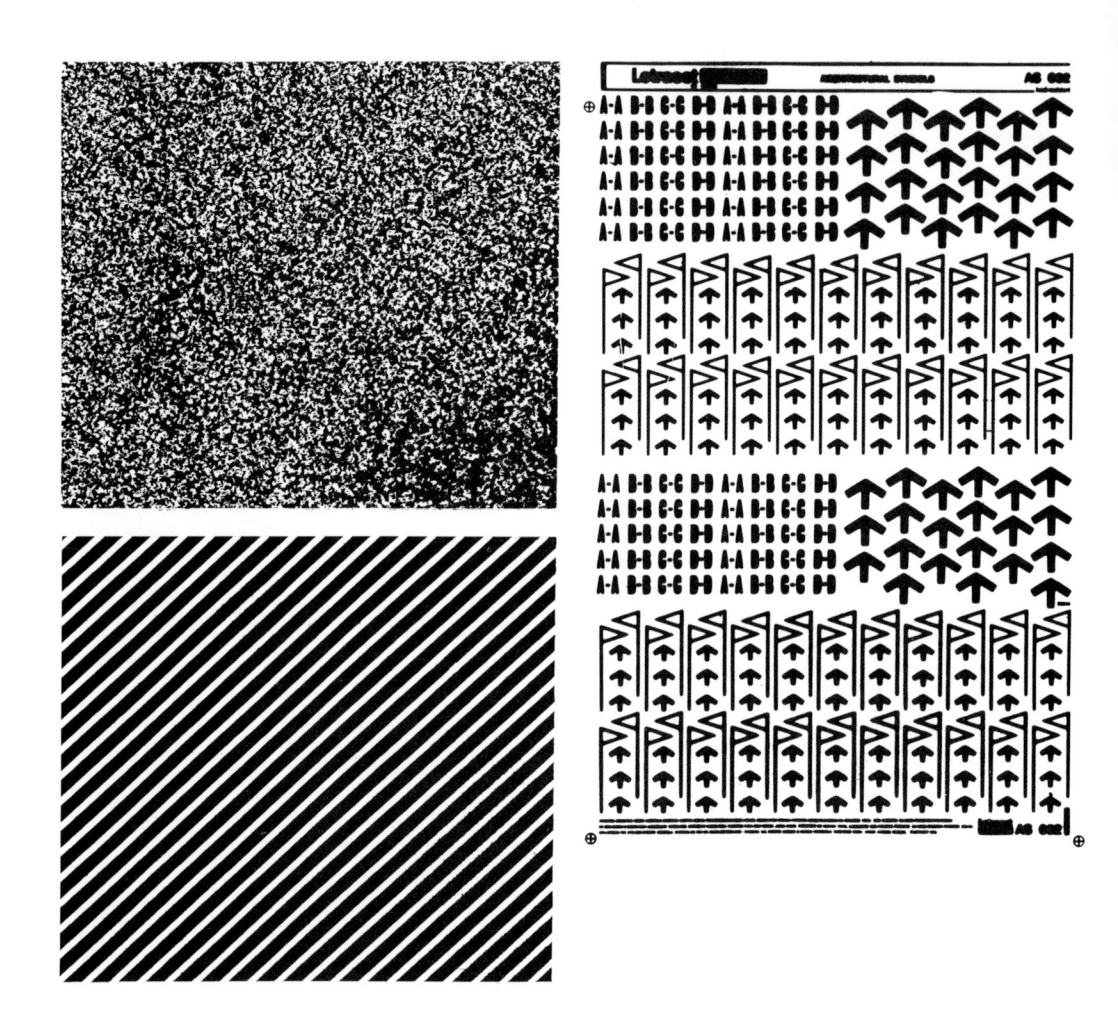

Now in case the reader thinks that here is the answer to all his problems, it must be pointed out that this method of lettering is very expensive for the *casual user*. It is only when the lettering is costed alongside the salary of the artist and the consequent saving of time, talent and temper that its use becomes demonstrably cheap. However, there are times when it is one of the possibilities we must consider. When, for instance, quality is the overriding factor, when the finished article is permanent and the cost can be spread over a period or when the ground for the lettering is unusual, this may well be the cheapest way of doing it.

The manufacturers will supply first-rate catalogues of the full range of their products, which runs from dozens of faces of type in many different sizes, through useful signs, symbols, drawings, sheets of half-tones, sheets of opaque coloured card and transparent film to large letters for indoor and outdoor display purposes. The range is, in fact, so immense and so much of it is outside our immediate frame of reference that it is best left to the manufacturer to explain.

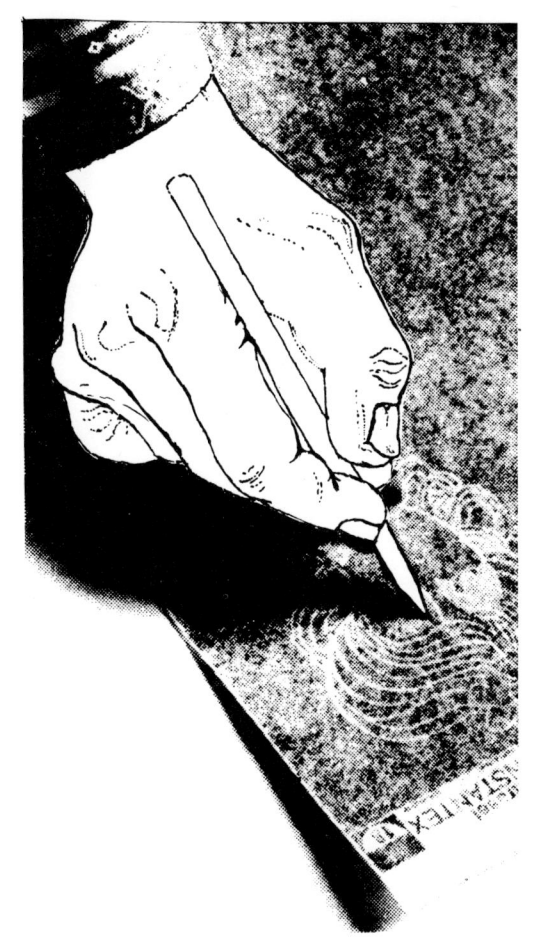

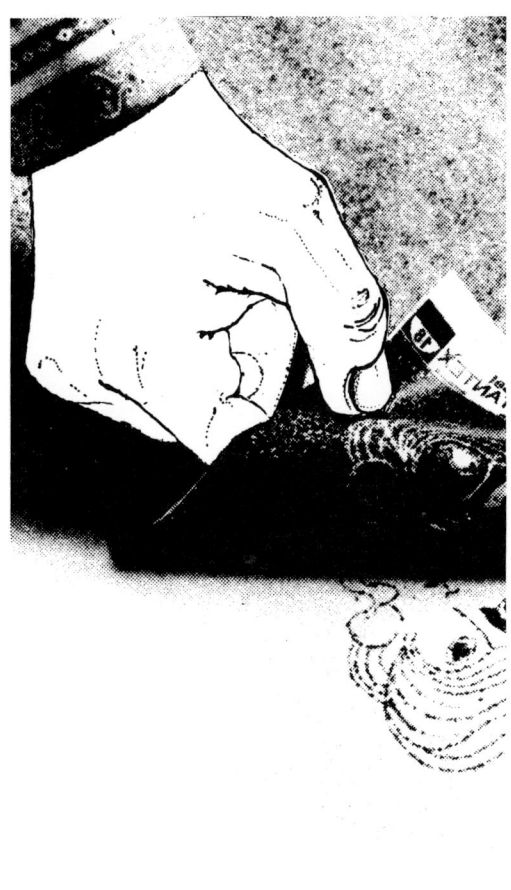

The use of instant lettering is now so widespread amongst designers that it is becoming easier to spot when it is *not* being used than when it is. Book jackets, cake boxes, commercial vehicles and motorway signs all display evidence of the use of instant lettering at the design stage. Clearly, the advent of a press-down letter of such a standard that it is ready there and then to be presented either to the client as a 'rough sketch' or to the printer as the finished article, has been of enormous importance to the commercial artist. It frees him from the most tedious part of his job and at the same time puts into his hands an extraordinarily versatile tool. This is why this form of lettering is used extensively in commercial art studios, television graphics studios and anywhere a high standard of lettering is required.

Instant lettering is, however, only part of the 'system' offered by the manufacturers. Also available are sheets of half-tones and textures in a bewildering variety, coloured background paper, coloured film, 'instant art' (sheets of drawings of people and bits of people), signs and symbols for architects, draughtsmen and electronics designers, 'body type' for layouts, protective coatings in aerosol cans and large letters for signwriters are some of these extra products. They are well worth considering as aids to the production of highly finished diagrams and charts. Two of the more unusual properties of instant lettering are that firstly it is now obtainable in transparent colours, mainly designed for use with the overhead projector, but useful for putting on to glass for backlighting, and secondly it is possible to obtain a limited range of type *printed backwards* for use on the inside of glass, effectively putting the lettering out of the way of curious fingers. In normal use, instant lettering needs no further protection. There are times, however, when the lettering may be rubbed, as when in use on instrument dials or on bottles or cans, and it is wise to use the added precaution of either spraying the work with one of the proprietary aerosol sprays made for this purpose, or covering it with a transparent varnish or clear polyurethane. You could even cover the whole job with a piece of transparent self-adhesive plastic of the sort found under such trade names as 'Fablon' or 'Transpaseal'.

I have already indicated that instant lettering may be used on virtually any dry surface. On rough surfaces a 'pre-release' technique may be used. Hold the lettering sheet away from the surface and rub lightly over the surface until the letter turns grey. Then place the letter carefully into position and press down with the finger. Burnishing must be done with some care, otherwise the letter may break up. Even the manufacturer would admit, however, that it is not often one would wish to put lettering on brick or rough timber, for example, with any hope of permanence!

It might be useful at this point to indicate some of the uses of instant lettering. This is not by any means a comprehensive list, but it may trigger off other ideas in the mind of the reader. Many of these uses could, of course, also apply to the other lettering methods suggested in other chapters.

Clubs and schools
Charts, notices, posters, visual aids, layouts for the printer for the school play, Open Day or Speech Day programme cover; shelf labelling in the library and laboratories; the library classifications chart; bottles, jars, cupboard and apparatus labelling; the 'Examination in Progress' notices used so regularly; 'Ladies' and 'Gentlemen' for appropriate doors for Speech Days (are *your* doors labelled, or does everyone just *know* which is which?); class numbers, teachers' names, 'On Duty Today' slide-in cards; the montage or 'paste-up' of components such as type, typescript and diagrams prepared for the photo- or heat-copier; simulation games-making at all levels and file identification are some things to be getting on with, but it is possible to read 'domestic science rooms' for 'laboratories' and 'art room' for 'library' in the above list, and add 'Pre-School Play Groups' and 'Young Wives Associations', 'Women's Institutes' etc. to the heading. . . .

Home
Labels on bottles, jars, cans in the kitchen, model aeroplanes, files, fuse identification, house names and numbers. Hobbies need labels, identification marks and numbers; still and cine photography need titles (remembering that one can use unusual surfaces or glass which can be lettered and used for super-imposition effects); home-made instruments need lettering for function and appearance (hi-fi amplifiers and radios) and model trains and boats can be given that professional touch with some of the very small lettering. Anyone who has ever needed to trace letters on to cloth before embroidering could well try instant lettering instead.

49

Restaurants, hotels, clubs and pubs
Notices (what about replacing those 'sandwiches on sale at the bar', 'no cover charge tonight' or 'all guests must be signed in' notices with some that look as though you care?); signs on doors and windows or directional signs (perhaps on frosted glass lit from behind); instructions to staff or customers. Cloakroom pegs can be numbered in ways other than by sticking pink tickets next to them, and key hooks and pigeon holes with hand-lettered labels look so *temporary*.

Offices and shops
Signs, notices and nameplates, instructions, directions, files and filing cabinets, reports, window displays, van lettering, ticketing, fixture labelling; direction, area and personnel identification.

Industrial, theatrical, commercial and electronic fields, as well as commercial design studios, medical and photographic businesses are normally serviced by professional designers and are, therefore, outside the scope of this book.

PRINTING

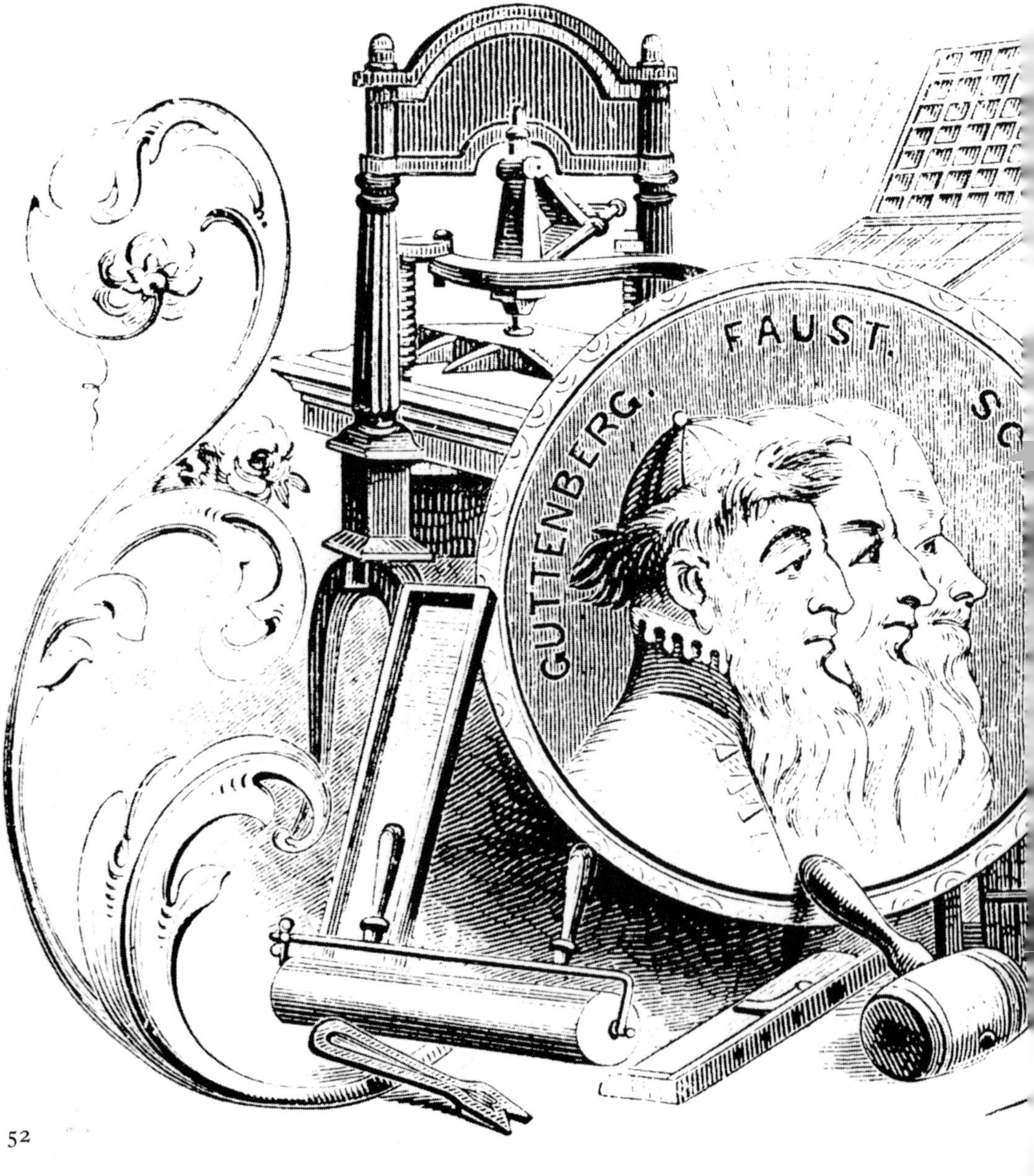
GUTTENBERG.
FAUST.
SC

The fifteenth century invention of movable type is one of the great landmarks in the history of man. Methods of printing had been known for three or four thousand years before then and the Chinese had a history of block printing and paper making long before Europe learned these skills. The traditional Chinese script, unfortunately, has many thousand separate characters which makes it a most difficult language to print. This is probably why movable type as we know it was first fully developed in the west where we have only twenty-six characters.

In about 1450, a German master printer named Gutenberg made a set of moulds from punches and manufactured large quantities of individual letters from each mould. He then had a means of setting up enough words to print pages of text at one go, and of re-distributing and re-using the same letters for the following pages or even books. Nowadays, machines are available which will do this with the speed of the typewriter, in which whole lines are cast instead of individual letters. Even more recent developments mean that we will see the end of movable type in its present form during the next two decades in the field of newspaper production and more generally by the turn of the century, as electronic and photomechanical methods take over.

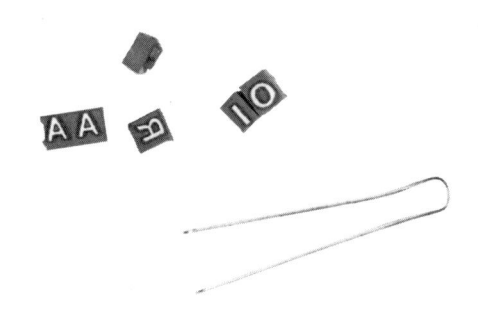

To most people the word 'printing' conjures up large inky-black machines, paper by the ton and copies by the thousand, whereas I am still thinking in terms of the single print. The easiest form of movable type for printing on a small scale is made of rubber. This is available from commercial suppliers in a small variety of sizes and styles. The letters are arranged in order in a holder of the appropriate size, inked on an office-type stamp pad and pressed on to the paper. Anyone who has ever used a child's

'John Bull Printing Outfit' will have no difficulty with this, as rubber type is simply a grown-up's version. This method is suitable for a limited number of bills, posters or notices or for many labelling jobs. Labels for shelves, filing cabinets, files, conferences, bottling and preserving are some of the uses that spring to mind. I have found it useful to set up a rubber stamp and try it out over a short period to see whether it would be worth while having it made up permanently by a rubber stamp manu-

Fig. 1

PLEASE NOTE

facturer. I am thinking of words like 'Processed' for film cans, order forms and files, where the same word has slightly different meanings, or 'today' for price labels, action files, the day's instructions to staff or personal memoranda. Like any form of movable type, rubber type is infinitely re-usable and its initial cost must be calculated as being spread over, say, ten years. Fig. 1.

Rubber type has one great advantage over other forms of printing in that the ink

Fig. 2

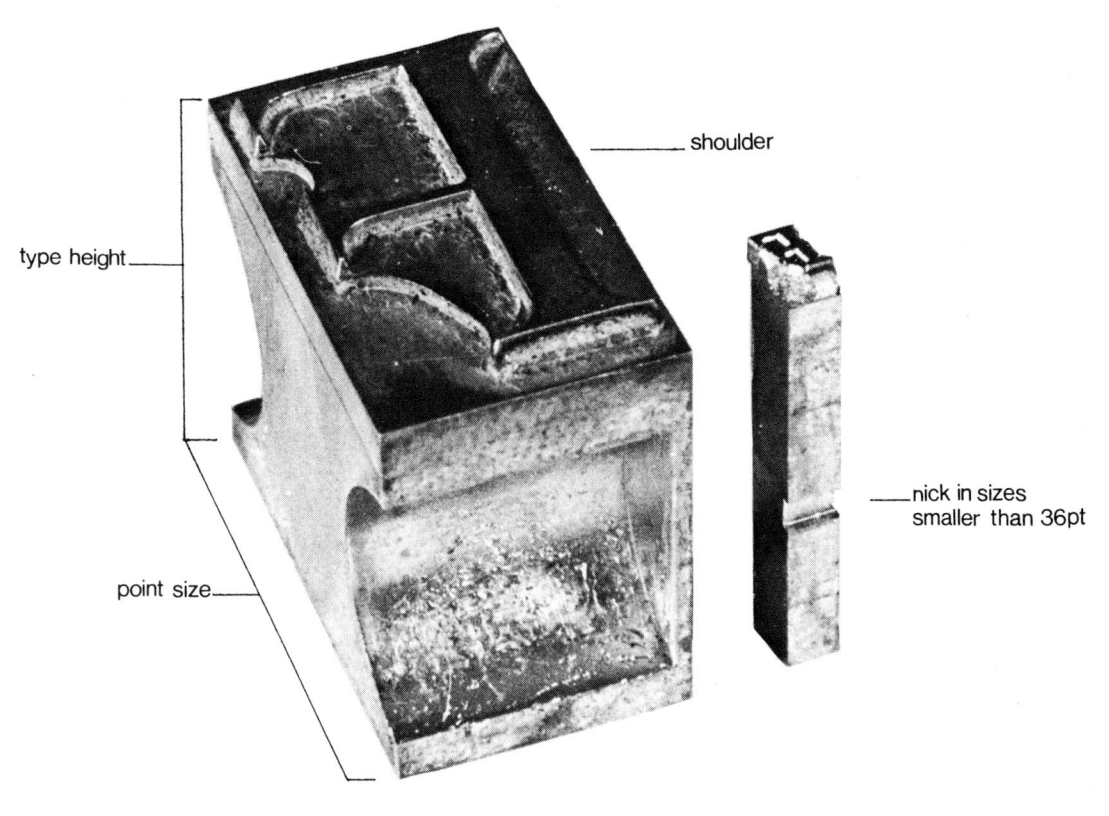

type height

shoulder

nick in sizes smaller than 36pt

point size

used is always ready in the form of a pad, but rubber type is not as accurate or as sharp as metal type.

A piece of metal type looks like this. Fig. 2.

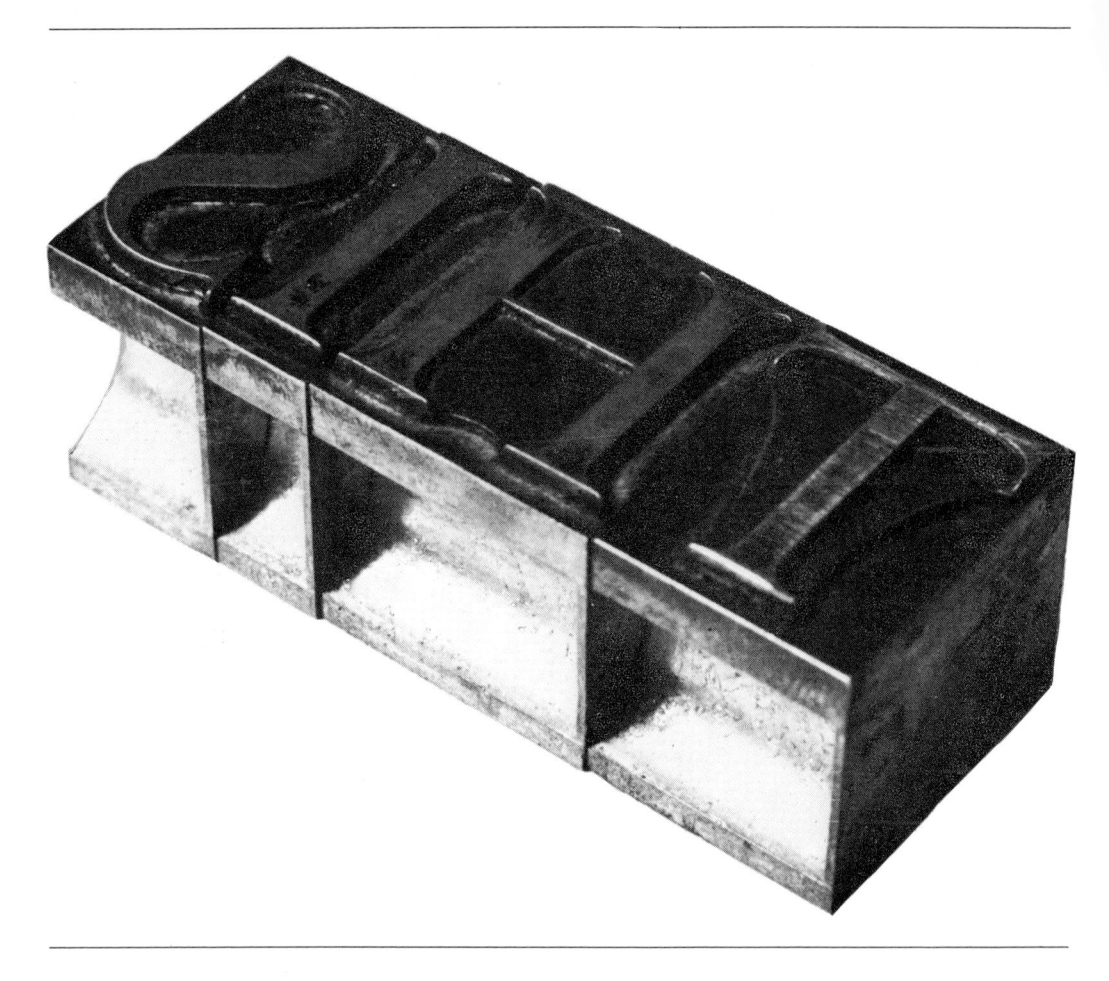

Several letters are placed together to form a word. Fig. 3 (above).

Ink is rolled over the lettering, Fig. 4 (above).

Fig. 5

Paper is brought into contact with the type, Fig. 5, and the print is pulled off, Fig. 6.

The lettering is cleaned and replaced in the type box.

With practice, the time taken to print a single word like this is between two and three minutes. The method is quick, and acceptable prints can be made first time, getting better as one practises *inking up*, which largely controls print quality.

Again, considering the number of times it can be re-used, it is surprisingly cheap in the long run. It should, however, be handled with care. The metal used in type-making is mainly lead and if you drop it you will either ruin the surface of the letter or distort the body so that it will not fit into the line.

Fig. 6

6 point◉   5 lbs. A 60 A 30 a 180
THE ARTS OF FINE Printing are to arrange

8 point★◉   5 lbs. A 40 A 20 a 120
THE ART OF FINE Printing is to set

12 point★◉   10 lbs. A 40 A 20 a 120
THE ART OF Fine printing is

10 point★◉   10 lbs. A 65 A 35 a 180
THE ART OF Fine printing is to

14 point◉   10 lbs. A 43 a 80
THE ARTS OF FINER Printing are to arrange type so

18 point★◉   10 lbs. A 30 a 50
THE ART OF FINER printing is to arrange

24 point★   10 lbs. A 14 a 28
THE ART OF Fine printing is to

30 point★   10 lbs. A 8 a 16
THE ART of fine printing

36 point★   10 lbs. A 6 a 12
THE ART of printing

48 point★   20 lbs. A 6 a 12
The Finest Arts

60 point   20 lbs. A 5 a 10
The Fine Art

72 point   20 lbs. A 3 a 6
The Finest

A B C D E F G H I J K L M N O P Q R S T U V W X Y Z & £ 1 2 3 4 5 6 7 8 9 0
a b c d e f g h i j k l m n o p q r s t u v w x y z . , ' : ; - ! ? ( ) fi ff fl ffi ffl
Also cast in 9, 11 and 42 point

62

When you come to buy your first type, and you open a type-founder's catalogue, you will find that the producers expect that you know what you are looking for and that you speak the same language as they do. I think I had better offer to translate some of the more frequently-used terms if you are not to be put off for good.

For instance, you will find that since printing is such an old and continuous craft it does not conveniently follow a system of measurement in feet and inches or millimetres, but has a method all of its own. This is based on a 'points' system, there being 72 points to the inch. If this seems simple enough, there is a catch. The points size refers to the dimensions of the body on which the letter is cast and not to the letter itself. A 72pt. letter is not one inch high, nor are two identical letters from different faces going to be exactly the same size as each other. There are two points systems, too, just to confuse things; Pica and Didot, but since

Fig. 7

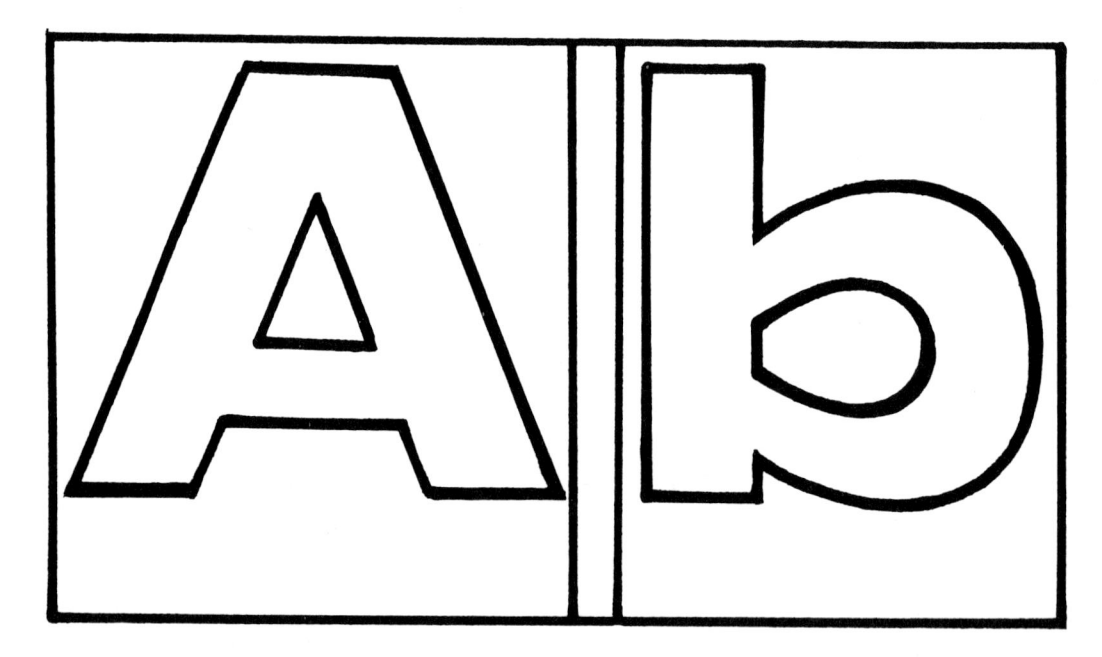

British type-founders mainly use Pica, this is of little consequence. The height of the type does not vary, being just under one inch total. The lower case 'x' is the standard letter of a face, but the size of this letter is determined by the length of ascenders and descenders. Fig. 7.

Type is available in sizes from 6pt. to 72pt. in metal; larger sizes are made from wood. It is despatched to the user in collections called 'founts', consisting of what at first glance appears to be a random and arbitrary number of letters, but which proves to be a carefully calculated distribution of often and little-used letters. Also included in the fount will be a complete collection of figures and punctuation in the same size.

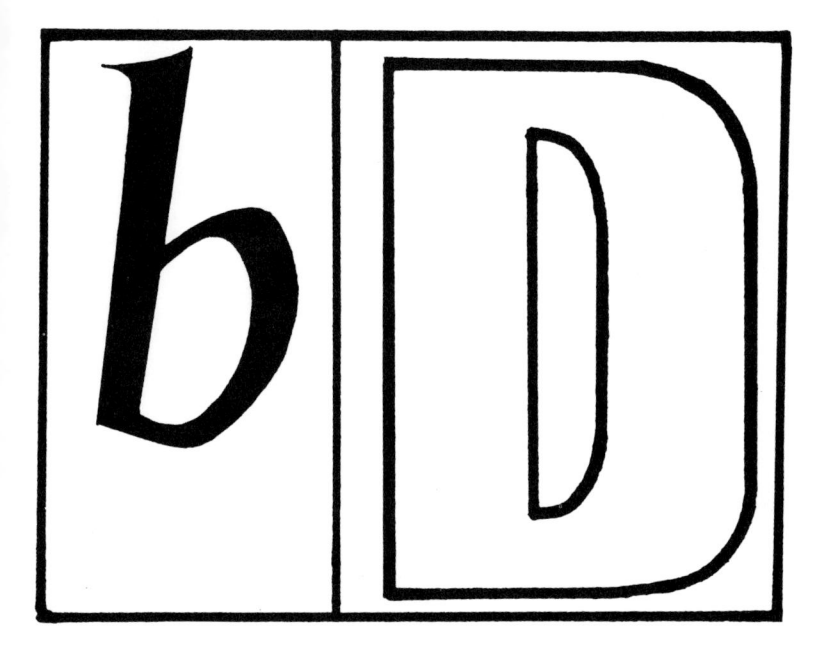

A specimen fount could consist of 12 capital As and therefore the following number of other capital letters:

B	C	D	E	F	G	H	I	J	K
5	8	7	14	6	6	7	12	4	4

L	M	N	O	P	Q	R	S	T
8	7	12	12	7	3	12	12	12

U	V	W	X	Y	Z
7	4	5	3	5	3

and the following number of lower case letters, again based on 12 'a's.

b	c	d	e	f	g	h	i	j	k	l
5	7	8	16	7	5	8	12	4	4	8

m	n	o	p	q	r	s	t	u	v
7	12	12	5	3	12	12	12	6	4

w	x	y	z
5	3	5	3

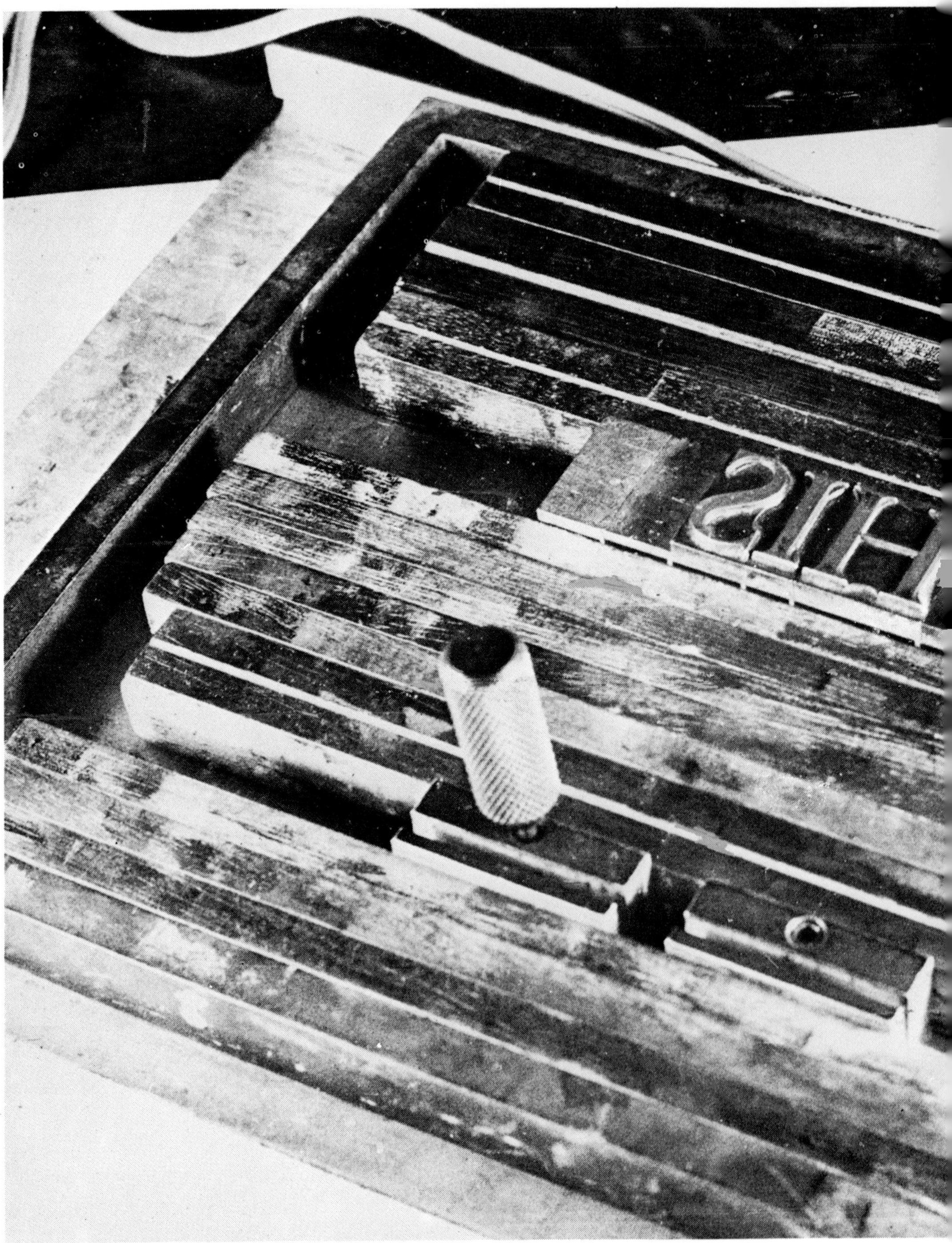

An appropriate number of punctuation marks (12 each of full stops and commas, for example) is included along with figures and, where necessary, combinations of letters like fi, ffi, fl, ff, ffl, Æ, Œ, £ and &. An initial fount of capitals based upon 3As, with the number of other letters scaled down proportionately, in a 36pt. size will be found to do a surprisingly large number of jobs, and will cost between two and three pounds.

In order to obtain suitable distances between words, you will need spacing pieces. They are in the same body size as the fount but are lower in height than the shoulder. Longer spaces, called 'quads' are useful for packing and filling in when larger distances are required between words, or when two or more lines are being set.

To stop the letters falling apart when they are being printed the type is placed in a metal frame called a 'chase' and packed together, or 'locked up' with pieces of wood called 'reglet'. The final locking up would be tedious if one had to rely on finding precisely the right pieces of reglet to squash the letters together, so you can buy or make wooden wedges. These push together to hold the type firmly in place. Even more conveniently, you can buy metal devices called 'quoins' (pronounced 'coins') which expand when a key is turned in the lock. Fig. 8 (left).

Ink can be bought from printers' suppliers (try Yellow Pages in the telephone directory for a local supplier if this is important) and is made in a wide variety

67

of colours. To roll out the ink you will also need a palette knife (an old kitchen knife will serve the purpose), a roller (buy the best you can afford and *keep it scrupulously cleaned* after each printing session) and a sheet of plate glass (an old car window or the glass fitted to some television sets do very well).

Arrange the type from left to right *upside down* and since p, b, q, and d can be confusing, the type-founder has cut a 'nick' in the body to indicate which way up the letter goes. When you scan a line of type, if all the nicks are at the bottom of the type, the letters are the correct way up. Fig. 9.

Remove a small quantity of ink from the tin and put this in the top corner of the glass. Spread a line of ink across the centre of the glass *the same width as the roller* Fig. 10 (right). Roll this out until it is the same size as the roller in both directions. Fig. 11.

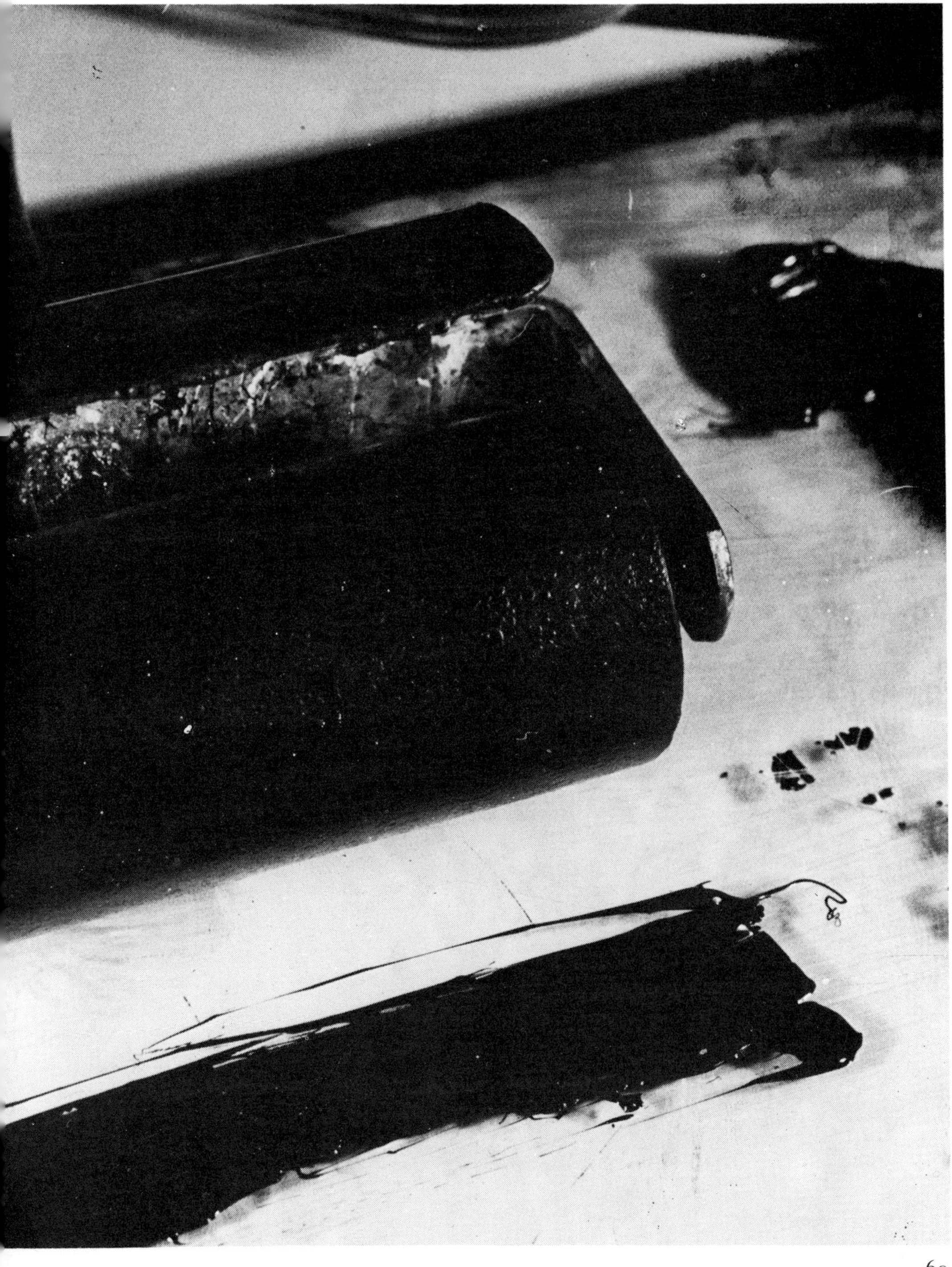

Fig. 11

There is no point in spreading the ink all over the glass, as the wider the ink is spread, the thinner it gets. The amount of ink needed is determined by experience. Try to listen to the *sound* the roller makes. If the ink 'slurps' there is too much of it, if no sound is heard, there is too little; the ideal is a muted silky noise. When you have found the ideal amount of ink, observe the surface and remember the sound. Roll the ink over the type evenly and carefully. Here again, practice will improve performance. Place the paper or card over the type carefully and *do not move it once it is in position*, otherwise the print will blur or smudge. If you are using a press, pull the roller over *once* and remove the print. If the print is not satisfactory, more often than not the inking is to blame. If using a hand roller to obtain the print, roll over the type area evenly and carefully and peel off the print evenly and carefully. This process is known as 'proofing'.

To obtain the best quality results, a press is required. Since this book is

Adana 'Five Three'

mainly concerned with one-off or very limited run jobs I shall ignore repeating presses, although it is fair to surmise that once you buy your first type, the possibility of a hobby often opens up and you wind up buying a small press from the Adana range. Professional proofing presses are fairly expensive, costing more than £50, but a smaller proofing press at about £18 is sold by Arnold of Leeds. I would recommend any school, college or institution setting up any sort of printing facilities for the first time, including string and lino prints, to go for the professional job as being cheaper in the long run. Second-hand presses are sometimes advertised in the classified columns of your local paper or publications such as 'Exchange and Mart'. If a press is not available a reasonable method is to use a clean roller. This requires a steady hand but can produce the results.

Smooth paper or card will render a sharper and cleaner print than a textured paper. Sugar, cartridge and ink duplicator

E. J. Arnold Mini-Press

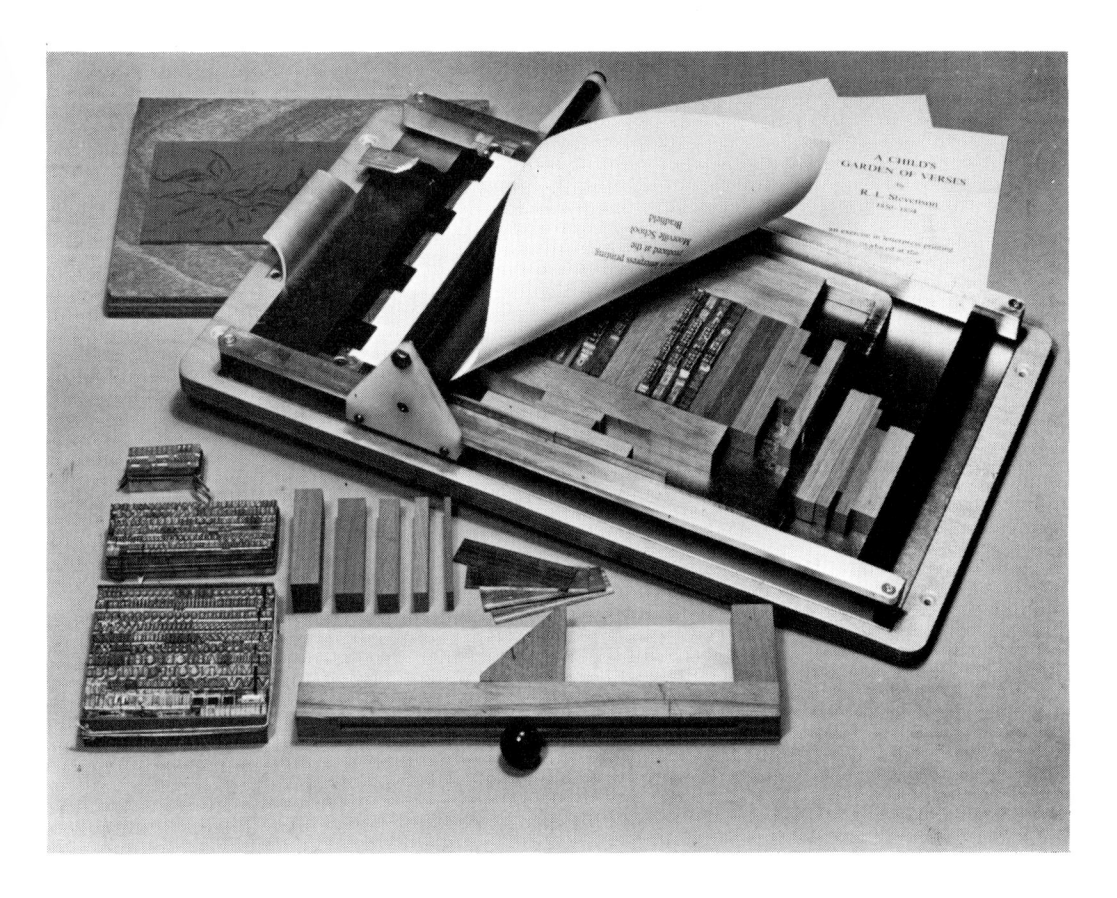

papers produce most disappointing results and are likely to put you off printing. Try a good bond paper or a thin (2 sheet) card for crispness.

Clean the knife, plate and particularly the roller most carefully with turpentine substitute or paraffin. Try to keep the roller in its delivery box. Since the best rollers are often made of gelatin, don't wash them in hot water or leave them standing on a window sill in the sunlight. They will melt. Also, stand the roller in such a way that the gelatin or rubber surface is not touching anything. The better rollers will have a guard or feet for this purpose. This avoids a 'flat' developing on the round roller surface.

At the same time clean the type with a cloth lightly damped with turps. or paraffin, and preferably use an old nailbrush to finish off. This is important, since ink is very similar in composition to paint or varnish, and dried up ink eventually begins to print with the type,

Fig. 12

obscuring detail and filling in small areas.

Type can be kept in cases specially built for the purpose. The arrangement of the printer's case for small-sized letters is completely baffling to the uninitiated, but for the larger 'Display' or 'Titling' faces of 36 to 72pt. a straight alphabetical arrangement is as good a way as any. Fig. 12.

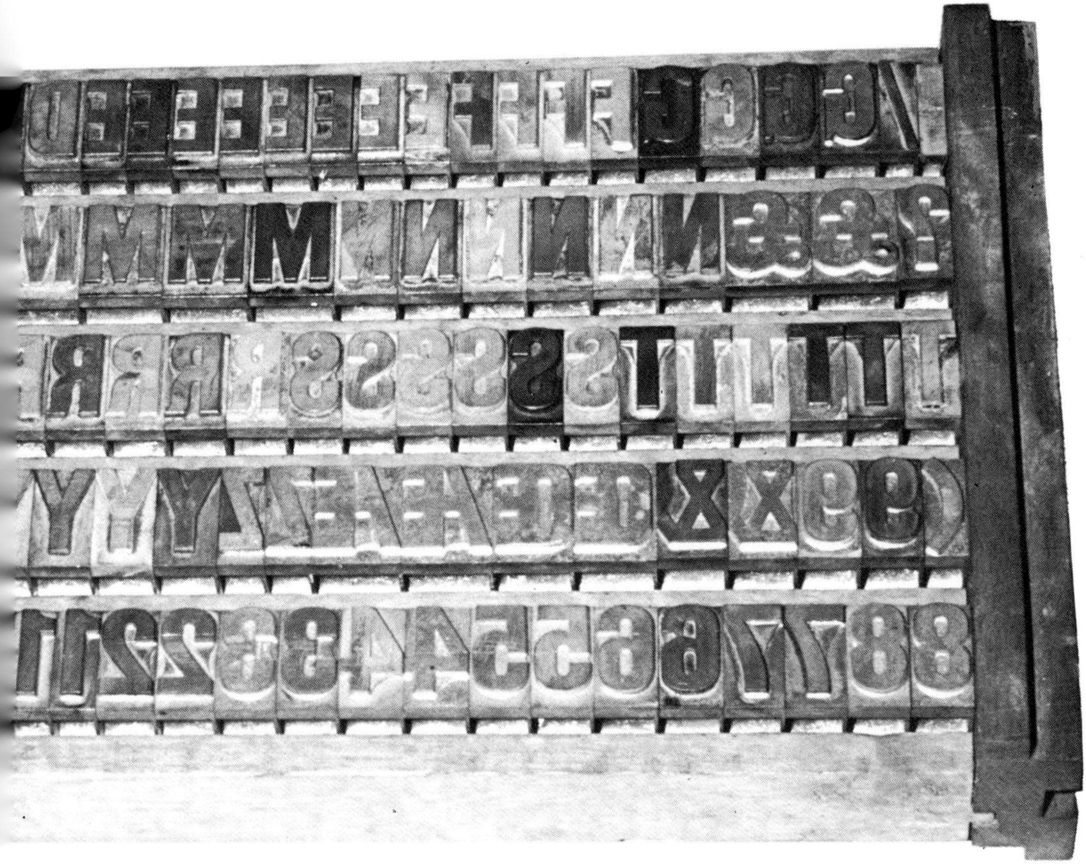

Fig. 13

THIS THIS
THIS THIS

Printing is obviously a way of producing excellent results, and is also a useful addition to a school's art and craft range, especially in conjunction with other forms of printing, in imparting a slick finish to book jacket and record sleeve designs. Youth Clubs, Community Centres, Parish Associations, Play Groups and the like sharing common premises could pool resources to purchase a small amount of equipment. A couple of founts useful for titling such as in Fig. 13 or any combination of two of these plus the necessary cases, spaces, quoins, reglet, roller, ink and press could be bought for about £30, which is why I have included it in this book as a realistic proposal.

LAYOUT

SUNNY STREET PLAY GROUP

BRING AND BUY SALE

To be held on Thursday, January 24th at 7.30 p.m.

Admission 2p

Artists have always lived by rules. From the time of the Renaissance there have been rules for proportion, colour, perspective and even for less tangible areas like harmony and composition. These rules developed over five hundred years until a century ago, when artists began to question them one by one. The nineteenth century artist, however, did replace each broken rule with one that he considered at least equally valid.

Now the world of art is divided sharply into two camps—the fine and the commercial. The fine artist struggles to sell his work and the commercial artist struggles to preserve his self-respect. All forms of art, however, interact. Painters and sculptors, commercial artists and photographers, architects, film makers and fashion designers learn from one another, adapt and influence one another's ideas until a style evolves which stamps the time in which they live.

With the ever-increasing speed of communication and the rapid turn-over in vogues, these styles change with bewildering rapidity and serve only to heighten the man-in-the-street's confusion and misunderstanding. The commercial designer and layout artist have the doubly difficult job of getting their message across in a form which their readers recognise and understand, and of satisfying themselves as artists.

CLIMBERS

> We have been trying to get this Club under way for the past two years, and we seem to have found a leader at long last.
>
> Mr. Godfrey will be here at the Centre on Friday evening next week to talk to anyone who is interested, and that means nearly everybody.

Fig. 1

Most of the books and magazines you will read, however, will be still firmly based on the design style of the 1950s and the early '60s, mainly because during that time there was a re-thinking of the basic elements of layout.

Try reading the announcement on page 78 quickly. This is a version of a handout which came through my door one morning. I have changed the words but the layout is the same. It seems to me that this is fairly typical of the amateur production at its worst, designed with the best of intentions, but totally lacking the discipline that the professional usually imposes upon himself. I am therefore going to propose a series of rules, which are there to be broken, but I would suggest you stick to them until you can replace them with better ones.

Rule 1
Always ask your reader to read from left to right. This is because we in the West read from left to right and from top to bottom, which is to say horizontally and vertically.

We rarely read in circles or diagonally, so we slow up when asked to read this way. Libraries are exceptions in that we expect to read book spines vertically.

Rule 2
Break up your poster or notice into blocks. Fig. 1.

Fig. 2

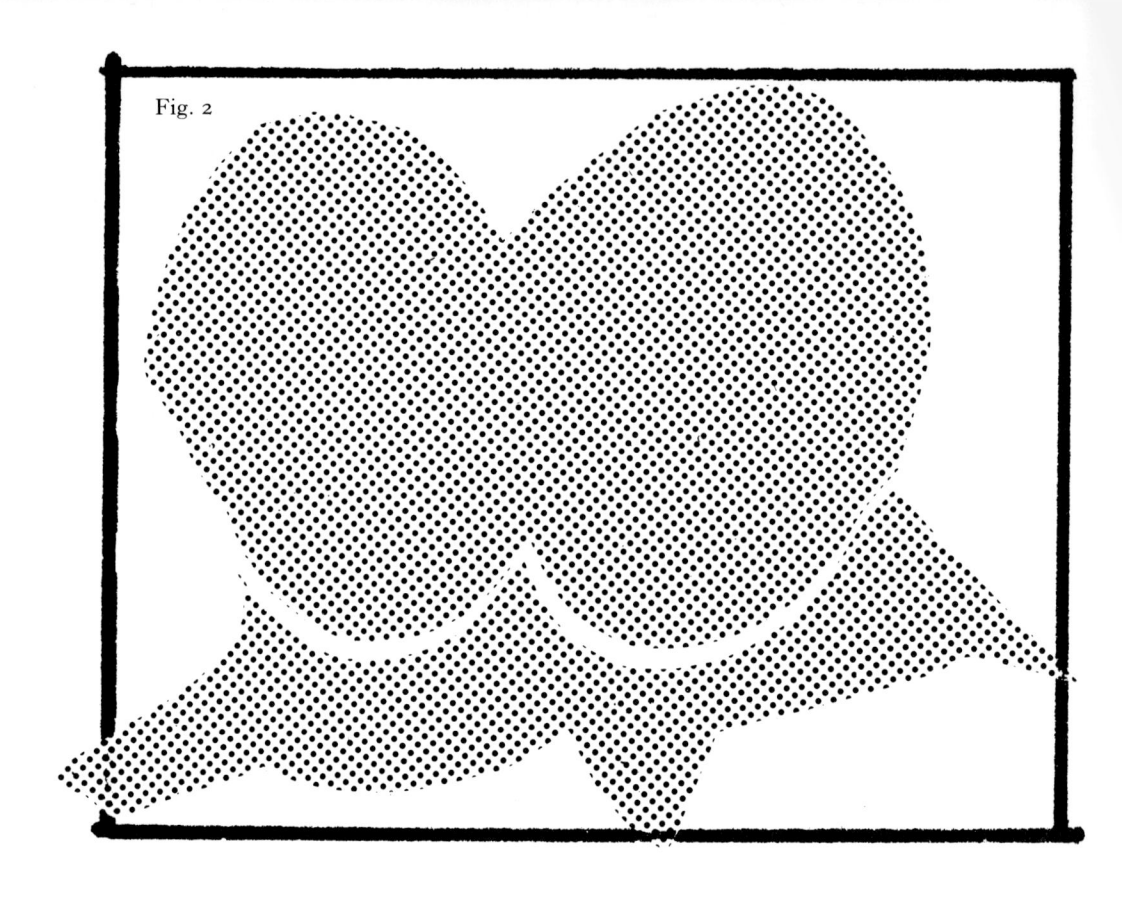

If you include a photograph or drawing, this will probably be in block shape already. Type can also be thought of in blocks, too. Put mental lines around words or groups of words. This will enable you to make an overall *design* from the *information* you have to impart, since people are so concerned about the words themselves they forget about the shapes those words are making. This will also help to keep information coherent and will prevent the designer arranging the words to fit a pre-conceived design.

Even irregular shapes can be thought of in this way. An imaginary rectangle around the shape turns it into a block. Fig. 2.

Rule 3

Arrange the edges of as many blocks as possible to follow imaginary vertical or horizontal lines.

When reading, our eyes have become accustomed, with practice, to reach the end of a line and move back very quickly to the beginning of the next line in much the same way that the typewriter carriage returns when beginning a new line. We expect this to begin directly underneath the previous one. By lining up the beginnings of lines in blocks, we are using this fact to its best advantage. Fig. 3.

thursday

a deserunt mollit anim id
gue nihil impedit doming
debit aut rerum
 endis dolorib asperiore
e cum memorite tum etia
tamen in busdam neque
s inflammad ut coercend
e fact· cond qui neg facile
sib conciliant et, aptissim
e ulla inura autend
 Itaque ne iustitial dem
luptat pleniore efficit. Tia
rtineren garent esse per
, ut mihi detur expedium.
idar et metus plena sit,
 despication adversantur
 spe erigunt

vident, simil sunt in culpa qui offici
um soluta nobis est eligend optio con
mporibud autem quinusd et aur office
hetury sapiente delectus ut aut prefer
dare torquat nost ros quos tu paulo an
tum poen legum odioque civiuda.
 on umdant. Improb pary minuit. potiu
fidem. Neque hominy infant aut iniust
conveniunt, da but tuntug benevolent
tat a natura proficis facile explent

ne aut sempitern aut diuturning timer naturan it salar'le grand. Auam
tra dicabit, dysa stante an movente propter legum ailman. Buoniam si
ede mus si movent. Tamen dicitis nulla turnen luptas erit praedermit
mpor incidunt ut labore et dolore magna aliquam erat voluptat.
 ex ea commodo consequat. Duis autem vel eum irure reprehenderit
r. At vero eos et accusam et iusto odio dignissim ducim qui

picurus a parvis petivit aut etiam a besti

Fig. 3

Fig. 4

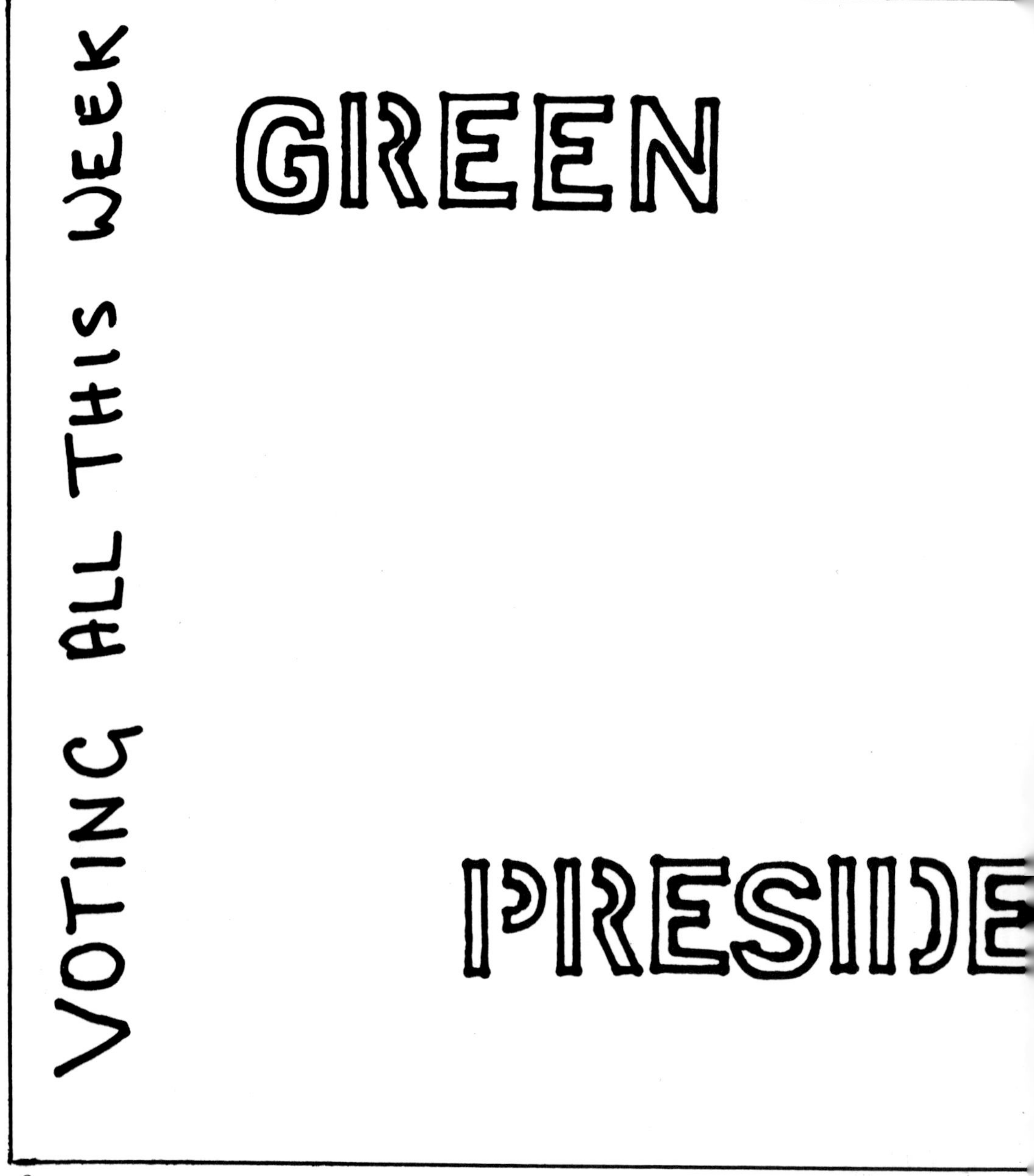

GREEN

VOTING ALL THIS WEEK

PRESIDE

Rule 4

Keep information as close together as possible.

There is no point in taking a large sheet of paper and attempting to fill it with small blocks. Either make the blocks bigger, get a smaller piece of paper or group all the blocks together. This gives a more easily digested arrangement which can be assimilated at a glance. The eye is not compelled to wander over several feet in order to get the message. If it is, at some point your reader will lose interest and you will have lost him for good. Figs. 4 and 5.

Fig. 5

GREEN FOR PRESIDENT
voting all this week

Fig. 6

Arising from this is the question of margins. How much space do you leave around the edges? The old proportions laid down that the smallest space went at the top, the next largest at the sides and the largest space was left at the bottom. Fig. 6.

This scheme is also based on a symmetrical arrangement on the paper, a style which can be followed or ignored, depending on the formality of the message. If you choose to replace symmetry with a less obvious arrangement, the choice is wide open. I would only suggest that you leave as much space around the edges as possible in order to avoid a cramped, mean feeling. Another alternative is to arrange the contents to reach right to the edges on one, two or three sides. When you produce asymmetrical arrangements, do so obviously, forcefully and with conviction. They won't work otherwise.

Whenever you place a shape on a piece of

Fig. 7

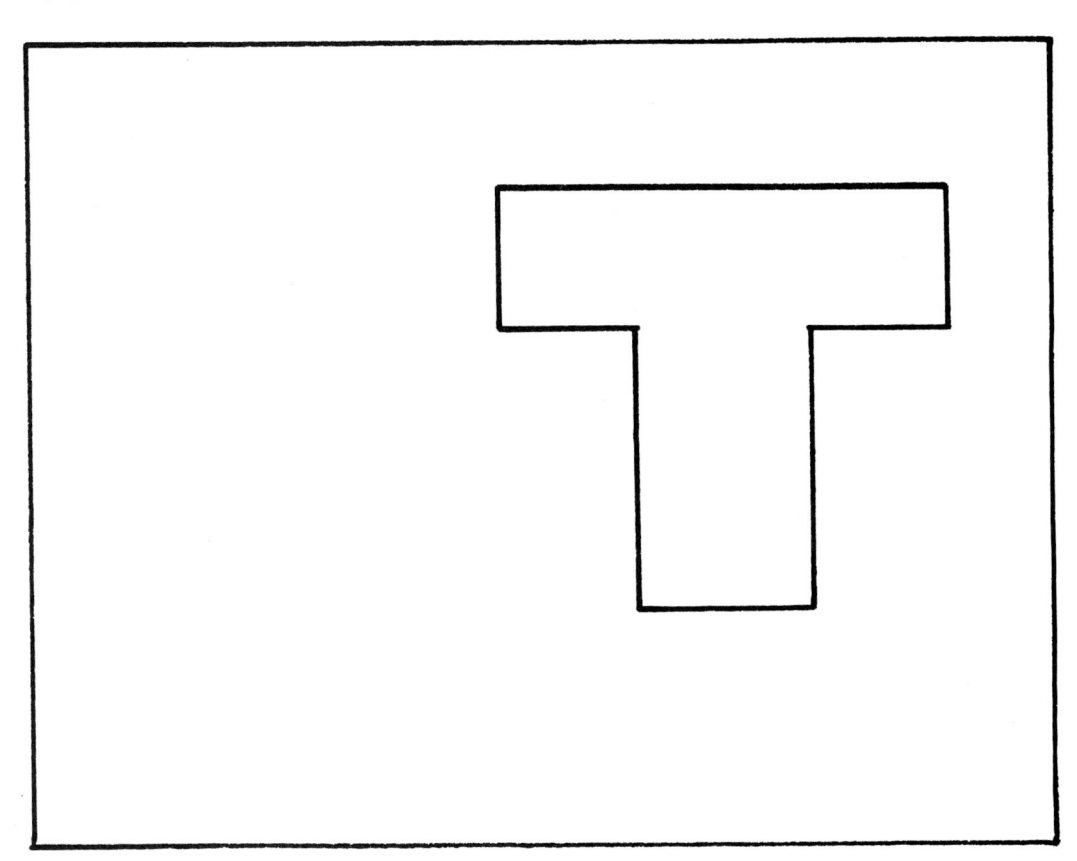

paper you are simultaneously *enclosing* some space and *excluding* other space. But since you are working within a third shape, the area of the paper, you are really creating two shapes at once, one within your line and one outside it. This is most important, since it means that you have to consider carefully the shapes you are leaving 'blank'. The artist refers to these areas as 'negative space' and they must be counted in the overall design. Fig. 7.

Rule 5
Remember to consider the negative space in your design.

This helps to make sense of Rule 4 and explains the logic of designs like Fig. 8.

I hope these suggestions are helpful. They are not by any means a complete guide to modern layout, but are offered simply as a starting point. Look around bookstalls and record shops at book jackets and record sleeves. Browse through magazines in your library. Some you will find stick to a traditional approach throughout, some are extremely adventurous whilst others have a mixture of traditional text layout and lively advertisements, or vice versa. 'The Gramophone' magazine, for example, has a fairly conventional text layout, but carries advertisements by the record companies which seem to have been designed specially for the magazine and which have kept up an extraordinarily high standard over the last twenty or so years that I have been reading it. If you want to see a practical demonstration of all the points in this chapter, and many more besides, obtain a current copy of this magazine. Many of the magazines aimed specifically at women adopt a very adventurous attitude to the layout of their pages. The general standard of photography and layout of their articles is of a very high order. In these magazines, too, you will come across the most delightful and unusual typefaces used with panache.

Use, copy, adapt and unashamedly steal the ideas you find for your own work. Gradually, by analysing every piece of layout coming your way, your sense of design will improve. Newspapers, letter headings, birthday cards and tax forms are all laid out by someone. What sort of job have they made of them? Has any thought been given to the layout or has the first solution that comes to hand been used? How would you have tackled it?

Fig. 8

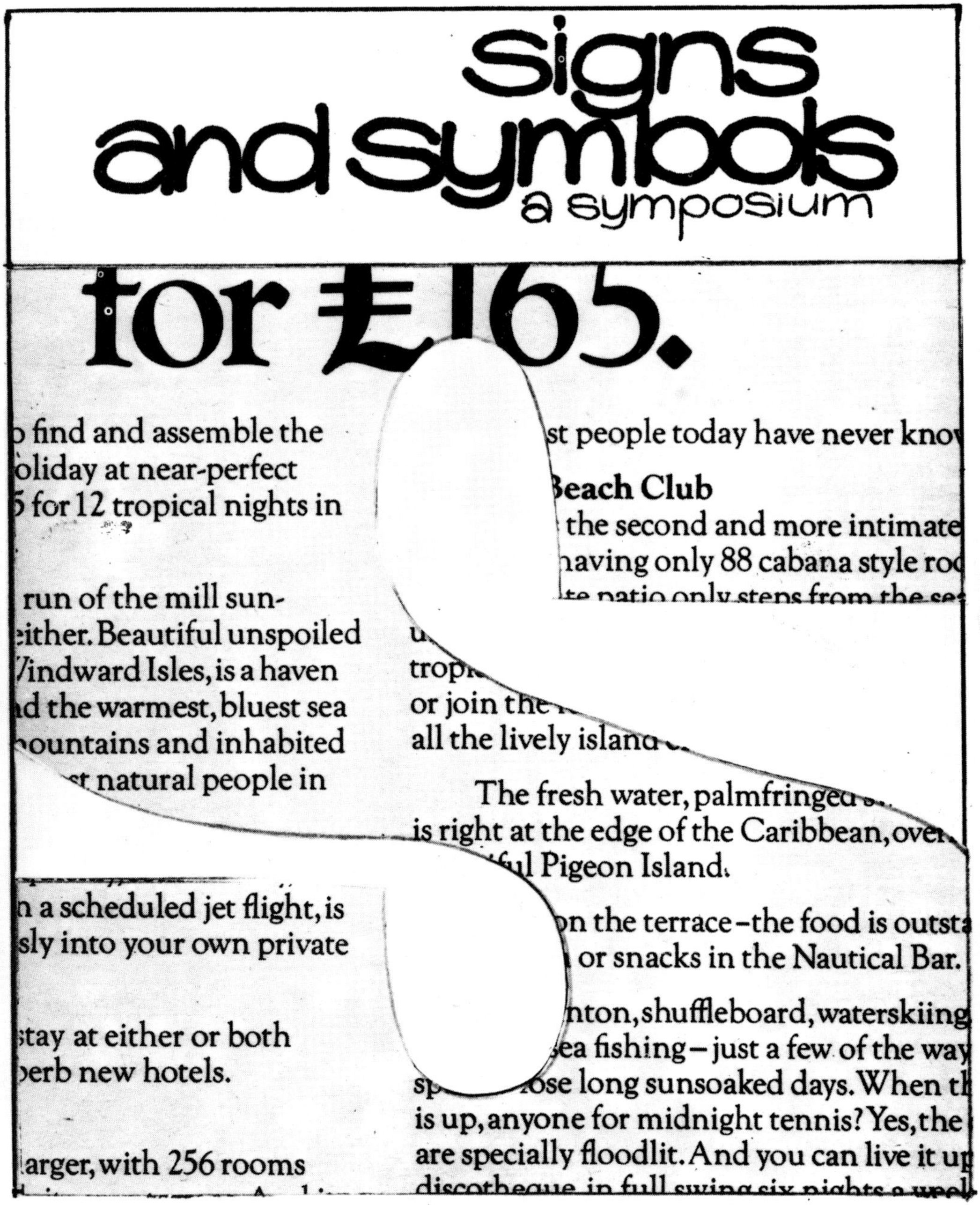

signs and symbols
a symposium

for £165.

find and assemble the
oliday at near-perfect
for 12 tropical nights in

run of the mill sun-
either. Beautiful unspoiled
Windward Isles, is a haven
d the warmest, bluest sea
ountains and inhabited
natural people in

a scheduled jet flight, is
sly into your own private

tay at either or both
erb new hotels.

arger, with 256 rooms

st people today have never know
Beach Club
the second and more intimate
having only 88 cabana style roo
te patio only steps from the se

tropi
or join the
all the lively island

The fresh water, palmfringed
is right at the edge of the Caribbean, over
ful Pigeon Island.

on the terrace – the food is outsta
or snacks in the Nautical Bar.

nton, shuffleboard, waterskiing
ea fishing – just a few of the way
sp ose long sunsoaked days. When t
is up, anyone for midnight tennis? Yes, the
are specially floodlit. And you can live it u
discotheque in full swing six nights a we

Fig. 9

Analyse the following illustration from a recent advertisement in 'The Gramophone' magazine. How is the design constructed? Do you agree with my suggestion? There are other ways of seeing it. Figs. 9 and 10.

90

Re-introducing to the catalogue

3 Beecham's Messiah
(Handel)

Jennifer Vyvyan, Monica Sinclair, Jon Vickers, Giorgio Tozzi
Royal Philharmonic Orchestra and Chorus conducted by
Sir Thomas Beecham Bart., C.

"There has been nothing like it before, and there will probably be nothing like it again. This is not the recording of the month, or even the year, but of the century."
D.S. *The Gramophone*—May 1960

4 records in box with notes and text £6.57 (usual price £10.00)
SER 5631/34

and on Victrola Sovereign for only 99p the first release in the Great Singers Series

The Art of Leonard Warren
(M)VIC 1595

The Met's First Butterfly (Excerpts)
Geraldine Farrar
(M)VIC 1600

Golden Age "Aida" (Excerpts)
Caruso, Gadski, Homer, Amato
(M)VIC 1623

RCA RECORDS AND TAPES

91

APPENDIX 1

Costs

I have included here some indication of the prices of the items mentioned in the text. Where more than one make is available, I have attempted to show the range of price variation. The prices are those current in 1973.

Item	Cost	Supplier (see Appendix 2 for addresses)
Writing tools		
Eagle felt pens. 12 colours available	$12\frac{1}{2}/14\frac{1}{2}$p ea.	1,3.
Fibre tip pens	$14\frac{1}{2}$p ea.	1,3.
Platignum Lettering set (fountain pen and 6 nib units)	74p	1.
Osmiroid Fountain pen with 6 nib units	94p	2.
Interchangeable nib units	13p	2.
Poster pens, 12 in a box, assorted sizes	35p	1.
Unograph pen	£1.40	6.
Poster pens } both illustrated in chapter 1, Fig. 26	31/41p per dozen	2.
Witch pens	9p ea.	2.
Stencils		
25mm and other varied sizes, waterproof paper	8p	4,5.
50mm, waterproof paper.	10/14p	1,5.
Econasign, comprehensive set	£4	1,8.
Plastic Letters, 50mm caps, fount	£1.05	1.
50mm lower case fount	£1.05	1.
Uno Stencils	from 30p	7.
Inks and diffusers		
Waterproof (can be used outdoors) 1oz.	$6\frac{1}{2}$p	1.
20oz.	52p	1.
5oz.	29p	5.
5oz.	23p	6.
Diffuser	11/14p ea.	1,6.

Item	Cost	Supplier
Instant Lettering		
Letraset, Letterpress, etc.	60p per sheet	9, 10, 11.
Type, accessories and press		
Dormy Red Face Rubber Type		
5A fount	£4.25	14.
72pt. Narrow Gothic. 3A caps, figures, points	£5.88	15.
36pt. Narrow Gothic. 3A caps, figures, points	£2.47	15.
36pt. Perpetua Title. 3A caps, figures, points	£2.47	15.
Cases to suit above. (see illustration, chapter 4)	£2.10 ea.	15.
Chase	£1.35	15.
Roller, 4½in.	87p	15.
Spaces, reglet, quoins and key, enough to begin with	£2.50	15.
Mini Press, bed size 13 × 9⅜in.	£18.90	1.
Coverings (see chapter 3)		
Fablon or equivalent, 18in. wide, per yard	24p	1.
Fablon or equivalent, 10in. × 10yds., per yard	90p	1.
Transpaseal, about the same thickness as Fablon, 20 × 30in. roll	20p	1.

APPENDIX 2

Suppliers (see Appendix 1)	Name and Addresses
1.	E. J. Arnold and Son, Ltd., Butterley Street, Leeds, LS10 1AX.
2.	Dryad Handicrafts, Northgates, Leicester, LE1 4QR.
3.	Margros. Eagle Pencil Co. Ltd., Monument House, Monument Way West, Woking, Surrey
4.	Reeves, Lincoln Road, Enfield, Middlesex.
5.	Geo. Rowney and Co. Ltd., P.O. Box 10, Bracknell, Berkshire, RG12 4ST.
6.	Winsor and Newton Ltd., Wealdstone, Harrow, HA3 5RH, Middlesex.
7.	A. West and Partners Ltd., 684 Mitcham Road, Croydon, CR9 3AB, Surrey.
8.	The Econasign Co. Ltd., 19/20 Palace Street, Victoria, S.W.1.
9.	Letraset, Ltd., 17–19 Valentine Place, Webber Street, London, S.E.1.
10.	Hunter Penrose Littlejohn Ltd., Longford Trading Estate, Thomas Street, Manchester, M23 0LP.
11.	Rexel, Ltd., Gatehouse Road, Aylesbury, Bucks.
12, 13.	Not mentioned in text, but included because they supply lettering for 'professional applications', made from cork and plastics. Very easy to handle and reasonably priced.
12.	Morol, Ltd., Gresham Road, Staines, Middlesex.
13.	Pintype and Moulded Letter Co., 51 Lisson Grove, London, N.W.1.
14.	Dormy Ltd., 27 Hoxton Street, London, N.1.
15.	Adana Printing Machines Ltd., 15–19 Church Street, Twickenham, Middlesex.

Suppliers	Name and Address
16.	(Type-founders, should you need larger amounts or single pieces of type). Yendall and Co. Ltd., Riscatype Head Office, Risca, Monmouthshire.
17.	Not mentioned in the text, but a similar firm to Nos. 1–6, supplying a wide range of lettering and allied products.
	Matthews Drew and Shelbourne Ltd., 78 High Holborn, London, W.C.1.
18.	Stencils, similar to Supplier 7. Standardgraph Sales Co. Ltd., 68 High Street, Chislehurst, Kent.

Some suggestions for further reading and reference.

For sample faces and master copies for use with chapter 1:
Lettera 1 and Lettera 2, by Haab and Stocker, published by Niggli. Lettera 3, by Haab and Haetenschweiler, published by Tiranti.

For reading on colour, a choice of three books:
The Colour Primer (the colour system of Wilhelm Ostwald, possibly the easiest to understand) ed. Faber Birren.
A Grammar of Colour (the system of Albert Munsell) ed. Faber Birren.
Principles of Colour (A review of colour theory) Faber Birren. Elements of colour (the colour system of Itten) ed. Faber Birren. All three published in the same series by Van Nostrand Reinhold.

For a more craftsmanlike approach to printing than this book contains:
Typography – Basic Principles (paperback) John Lewis. Published by Studio Vista.

An Introduction to Printing. Published by Adana. (Leaflet L 1403) The Beginner's Guide to Design in Printing. L. G. Luker. Adana.

General reading, particularly useful for students:
Communications Graphics. M. P. Murgio. Published by Van Nostrand Reinhold Co. 1969.

Audio-Visual Methods in Teaching, Edgar Dale. Published by Holt, Reinhart and Winston, Ltd., 1969.

Ideas, Inspiration, Layout:
Basic Design – The Dynamics of Visual Form. Maurice de Sausmarez. (paperback) Published by Studio Vista.
Graphic Design, by Fletcher, Forbes and Gill. (paperback) Published by Studio Vista and highly recommended.

The Modulor. Le Corbusier, translated by De Francis and Bostock. Published by Faber and Faber.

Graphis Annual, ed. Herdeg. Published by the Graphis Press, Zurich. Modern Publicity, ed. Gluck. Published by Studio Vista.

Finally, if you want to see what a really modern layout looks like, try Visionary Cities – the Arcolgy of Paolo Soleri, by D. Wall. Published by Praeger Publishers, Inc.